Lakes, Lures and Lodges

Lakes, Lures and Lodges

An Angler's Guide to Western Canada

By Jake MacDonald

Illustrations by Luther Pokrant

Turnstone Press

Turnstone Press
607-100 Arthur Street
Winnipeg, Manitoba
Canada R3B 1H3

Cover photographs: Gordon Pyzer

Illustrations: Luther Pokrant

Text design: Manuela Dias

This book was printed and bound in Canada by Kromar Printing for Turnstone Press.

Canadian Cataloguing in Publication Data

MacDonald, Jake, 1949–

Lakes, lures and lodges

ISBN 0-88801-176-8

1. Fishing – Canada – Guidebooks. 2. Fishing lodges – Canada – Directories. 3. Fishes – Canada. I. Pokrant, Luther, 1947– II. Title.

SH571.M25 1993 799.1'0971 C93-098202-9

Table of Contents

Family Fishing Resorts

Eating Them

Dwindling Resources

Appendix

How to Use This Book

We've organized the book by species. Each popular gamefish gets its own chapter. In each one we provide information on the fish – its diet, breeding habits, and behaviour. We also tell the story of lures famous for catching each species. Best of all, we take you fishing at the best places in western Canada for catching nine top species of gamefish.

We've also provided a special section on "Family Fishing Spots." This chapter describes a range of excellent, inexpensive places across western Canada where you can enjoy a family vacation and still partake of hot fishing at the same time.

Of course there's nothing better at the end of a long day on the water than a delicious meal of fresh-caught walleye, trout, or salmon. So we've included a chapter called "Eating Them," which describes a number of jealously guarded recipes, outdoor cooking methods, and pro fishing guide techniques for making the best fish meal you've ever had.

Finally, a chapter entitled "Dwindling Resources" examines some of the issues affecting the sport – changing ethics, declining fish population, and the growing popularity of catch-and-release fishing.

The Appendix at the end of the book provides names, phone numbers and addresses of some of the best outfitters, lodges, and campgrounds in western Canada.

PREFACE

In the spring of 1488, on a dark blustery wet evening in the English countryside, a horse clattered in through the gate of Sopwell convent, near St. Albans. The rider, a woman in a hooded cloak and sturdy shoes, slipped off the horse and detached a bag from the saddle.

After tiptoeing up the stairs to her quarters, she loosened the lacing on the bag and emptied a number of items onto the pantry table . . . knife, collapsible fishing rod, feathers, line, metal hooks, and a fine, glistening trout. Later, after dinner, she sat at her desk under a flickering lantern and worked at her epic manuscript, *A Treatyse of Fysshynge Wyth an Angle*. Her name was Dame Juliana Berners. She worked a day job as a nun. But her true passion was fishing. Dame Juliana Berners did not exactly invent fishing, but she was the first educated person to take it seriously.

Juliana Berners' text, which was finally published in 1496, is the first comprehensive work on the gentlest of the blood sports – angling. Although followed by other great works like Izaak Walton's *The Compleat Angler*, Dame Juliana's book first introduced the notion of angling as a complex, silent, contemplative pursuit that teaches patience, dexterity, aesthetics, the laws of nature, physics, fish biology, and many other skills, with the whole exercise rounded off with a tasty feast. Since that time, five hundred years ago, angling has grown into one of the most popular and respected of outdoor pursuits. In North America, billions of dollars are spent every year on fishing tackle, licences, and boats. The sport has generated TV shows, seminars, mail-order videos, and a class of pro anglers who spend much of the year travelling in pursuit of big cash purses at fishing tournaments across the continent.

Yet despite all the hustle, fishing still calls for a lone angler and a great big stretch of silent water. The rewards are still clean air, nature's beauty, and a delicious meal at the end of the day. In an era of unfriendly cities and dwindling natural spaces, angling's simple rewards are probably the real cause of the sport's growing popularity.

Canada, with less than one percent of the world's population, has more fresh water than any country on earth. And along with that abundance of lakes and rivers comes a remarkable wealth of wildlife and freshwater fish. After the First World War, small aircraft became commonly available and a new Canadian institution was established – the fly-in fishing lodge. With planes on floats, outfitters could bring their clients into lakes that were previously accessible only on foot or by canoe. Since most of Canada is wilderness still not road-accessible to this day, flying anglers continue to discover a whole new world.

There are several hundred fishing lodges in western Canada. For purposes of this book, that includes the western edge of Ontario. About half of the lodges are accessible by plane only. The rest have gravel roads. A few can be reached by modern paved highway. There's no shortage of information on the location and amenities offered at these lodges. Every winter, lodge owners travel the sports show circuit in the United States and anglers have a chance to meet the operators in person. But even at a sports show, a hundred booths, all festooned with photos of blazing sunsets and huge fish, may overwhelm the senses of some poor angler who's trying to answer a simple question:

"Which one of these places is a really good, dependable place to go fishing?"

A simple question, perhaps. But as we all know, there's nothing more elusive than the answer to a simple question. Government tourism officials are swamped with enquiries from anglers who want qualitative judgements on the best lodges, but government people aren't allowed to recommend one lodge over another. Taxidermists receive physical evidence of where the big fish are being caught, but they too are reluctant to make enemies amongst the lodge owners. Bush pilots, equipment suppliers, financial institutions, lodge employees, and many others are good potential sources of comparative information, but those who are close to the business have good reason to keep their mouths shut.

In private, all of these groups, even the lodge operators themselves, will speak frankly about who runs the best fishing camps. But the average angler is not likely to overhear these little nuggets of inside information. Faced with a blizzard of brochures, maps, price lists, photos, and sales-banter from lodge owners, the average consumer is likely just to throw up his hands and rely on the advice of his cousin Ernie.

The lodges described in this book were chosen on the basis of many off-the-record interviews with tourism officials, air charter operators, game wardens, taxidermists, veteran anglers, biologists, guides, and lodge owners themselves. Surprisingly, when the last drink is served, there is very little disagreement about which are the best fishing camps. In fact, some of the lodges profiled in this book were recommended, albeit grudgingly, by rival operators.

We've organized the book by species, with pike, walleye, muskellunge, and the other popular gamefish species getting a chapter each. A small number of very good lodges were selected as the best places to catch these species. In many cases, lodges were left out because there was only room for a handful of camps to go with each species. In other cases, lodges were not mentioned because, instead of offering great fishing for one particular species, they feature good-to-excellent fishing for a whole variety (for example God's River Lodge and Grass River Lodge in northern Manitoba). In short, being excluded from this list may not mean much. But we can provide assurance that being included means that the lodges are exceptional. They provide a good, well-rounded package of great scenery, friendly service, dependable transportation, excellent food, comfortable lodging, and, last but not least, the best fishing in the world.

Most Canadian lodges emphasize catch-and-release fishing nowadays, as they should, but keeping a few fish for dinner is still an important part of the ritual. And I for one will probably hang up my rig comes the day that we are no longer permitted to kill a fish for dinner. After all, angling is just a process of feeding yourself, both spiritually and otherwise. And when all the frantic planning, the traffic jams, the sky-high prices, the plane rides, the always-overlooked final complications are dealt with, it still comes down to that same stretch of rocky shoreline, that same glassy, painted water, that same silvery loop of line curving out like a prayer. In the five hundred years since our patron saint Dame Juliana invented fishing, it is still "good sport and honest," as she once observed, "to see the fair, bright shining fishes deceived by crafty means, and drawn out upon the land."

If Dame Juliana was around today, here are some of the places she'd want to visit.

Northern Pike

NORTHERN PIKE

Esox lucius, also known as the "jackfish" in the Canadian north, occurs in northern regions around the world. In Europe, where the biggest pike have been recorded, the mythology of this fish goes back for centuries.

Named after an Anglo-Saxon battleaxe called the "pike," this fish was thought to have about as much delicacy as the murderous weapon that was its namesake. Feeding on frogs, ducklings, and almost anything else that fit in its mouth, the pike was a curiosity to medieval observers, who assumed that it grew to enormous size. Early accounts tell of swans, dogs, men, and even horses that fell victim to monster pike. Famous individual pike occasionally surfaced to bolster the legend. One monster, the Mannheim pike, was supposed to be 267 years old. Another famous fish was the Lake Kaiserwag pike, a mounted specimen rumoured to weigh 350 pounds. Perhaps the Greatest Fish Story Ever Told, the Lake Kaiserwag pike, in fact, turned out to be a whole series of pike mid-sections melded together to make a fish 19 feet long. In Bohemia, pike were raised in farm ponds as early as the 11th century, and their bones sold as charms to ward off witches. Like wolves, snakes, and other supposedly sinister animals, the pike has always symbolized the cold-hearted, predatory aspect of Nature.

Although the pike will strike aggressively at artificial lures much of the time, pike fishing is not always the slug-fest that outdoor writers describe. In the warm months of summer, when most anglers take their holidays, pike fishing can be extremely frustrating and unproductive. Warm water, diminished oxygen content, abundant baitfish, and the retirement of larger pike to deep water conspire to reduce the effectiveness of angling. Generally pike become less active in water that is warmer than 65°F. Keen pike anglers would be well advised to confine their activities to the cold water periods at either end of the summer season.

In spring or fall, fishing for northern pike is best early in the morning. Unlike muskellunge, northern pike do not feed at night and in the morning these fish wake to an empty stomach. Lures are a matter of personal preference, with flashy spoons (like the Len Thompson Five of Diamonds), wobbling shallow-running plugs (like the Rapala), and feathered spinners (like the Mepps No. 5) being the most obvious choices. While pike will strike at anything, an angler with a bit of finesse and imagination will catch many more pike than the one who grimly persists in the notion that the pike is a brainless thug that will hit anything in the tackle box.

A pre-game pep talk for northern pike fishing includes the following reminders:

1. **Choose a lure that will perform well** in the given situation. In heavy weeds, use a spoon or plug that will swim just above the weed tops.
2. **Go to a smaller lure** if pike are striking short or missing your lure. Don't be afraid to use a light, small spoon. Even large pike will strike a small lure.
3. **Always use a wire leader**. Walleye anglers using jigs will testify to the fact that pike will snip off a lure instantly, if it is tied onto monofilament line.
4. **Fish early and fish deep** in hot summer weather. Large pike spend the entire summer in deep water, foraging on ciscoes and other cold-water baitfish.
5. **Wear a light leather glove,** and bring fish into the boat by slipping your hand into their gills. Pike in a landing net create a horrible mess, and the fish are usually so entangled that it becomes difficult to release them in good time.

CAN FISH SMELL?

Northern pike, smallmouth bass, and most clear-water fish rely primarily on eyesight to hunt their prey. But all the same, most fish have keen senses of smell. A bass can smell one part per trillion, which is the equivalent of one drop of blood in 500,000 barrels of water. Pike, bass, trout and other sight-oriented fish may charge a bait, then pause momentarily before striking. At that moment, a dab of scent on a lure may make the difference between a missed strike and a hook-up.

In Europe, pike-fishing is a centuries-old tradition, and anglers in the England of 300 years ago often used scent for catching pikes.

"I still get cheesed off when I hear people call these fish 'snakes.' I've been to places like Japan, and you know what we're famous for? Big northern pike. They've only heard about northern Manitoba for that reason. So why don't we celebrate these fish? Why don't we recognize that we've got a world-class resource here?

We shouldn't call them snakes. These snakes are us."

—Trapper Don

How to Weigh A Northern Pike without a Scale

(use inches and pounds)

$$\frac{\text{length} \times \text{length} \times \text{length}}{3500} = \text{weight}$$

Dardevle Lure

A Lure to Beat the Devil

The Detroit of the late 1800s was a very different place than it is today.

No phones, no plumbing. No big auto plants churning out cars to fill the American freeways. After school, a kid could pick up a shotgun or fishing rod and walk down to the banks of the Detroit River to rustle up dinner. Canvasback ducks were so numerous that they swept past in swarms. And northern pike and walleye could be caught right off the shipping piers.

One of these youngsters was Lou Eppinger. Like most kids, Lou was expected to move into a trade apprenticeship as soon as he finished school. As coincidence would have it, he apprenticed with a taxidermist. When the owner died, young Lou took over the business.

Taxidermy was a not a fast-track career. During hunting and fishing season, Lou Eppinger managed to pay his bills. The rest of the time, he scrambled. But Eppinger enjoyed life. In an age when marriage was sacred he lived with his girlfriend, played poker in the back of the shop, swigged bourbon, and knocked off once in a while to go hunting and fishing with his pals. The birds that people brought in to be transformed into feathery objects for their parlours meant food for Eppinger and his sweetheart. He'd skin a couple of canvasbacks, Betty would put them in the oven on low heat, and they'd slip off to the racetrack. When they returned, their feast was all prepared.

On a solitary trip to Canada, Lou wandered for a month in the Ontario bush, amusing himself by trying to invent a lure that would catch fish. In 1906, there were essentially no modern lures in existence, and Eppinger didn't have much to go on. He experimented with different types of metal spoons, hammering them into various shapes, and finally came up with a very heavy (2-ounce) spoon that flipped back and forth rather than revolved when retrieved. The spoon was heavy and awkward, but at least he'd broken the spin barrier (spinning lures twist fishing line). Most importantly, the lure caught fish. Specifically, pike. Northern pike attacked his spoon with gusto, and there were enough pike that Eppinger could test each design innovation with his toughest critics – the fish. He took the lure back to his Detroit taxidermy shop and discovered that customers wanted to buy samples of it.

Eppinger continued working on the lure, sales picked up, and in 1918 he joined forces with his nephew Ed. Together, they decided to go full-time into the fishing-lure business. They also decided to come up with a catchy name for their spoon. The First World War had just ended, and many of Eppinger's friends had served in the USMC. The Marines had done well in the war, and in fact had been dubbed the "devil dogs" by their German counterparts. Americans turned the name around and began calling Marine veterans the "dare devils." Eppinger liked the sound of the name, and borrowed it for the new fishing lure.

Thus, the Dardevle was born. Because of patent laws, the spelling had to be changed: dictionary words could not be used in a trademark. The Eppingers were big believers in advertising, and sales rose as the lure began to appear in fishing magazines like *Field & Stream*. "Genuine Indian Guides Favor it in the Far North Woods of Canada!" exclaimed the ads. Sales climbed from 500 to 6000, and then higher. By 1928, the company was selling 50,000 lures per year. Today, Dardevle sales are still very strong, with the red and white model still being the most popular, and annual sales holding at around three million lures. The ads helped, but in fact the lure works like magic on the northern pike.

The traditional Dardevle is red, with a wavy white stripe, and the trademark face of Lucifer. If there's no devil face, it's not a Dardevle. Dardevles catch everything from saltwater fish to walleye, but they are still the ultimate lure for northern pike. As Lou Eppinger once remarked, "Pike made this company."

HUNTING for HATCHET-FACE

Where can you go to catch lots of big northern pike?

First, it's necessary to narrow the search down to a general region. Canada has the biggest pike in North America. But where to go in Canada? In most areas of southern Canada, northern pike in the 5-pound range are considered good-sized fish, and anything over 15 pounds is exceptional. To catch very large northern pike on a regular basis, it's necessary to travel to northern Manitoba or Saskatchewan, where anglers catch 20-pound fish almost every day, and where 25 to 30 pound fish are not rare.

According to some observers, pike grow so large in the north simply because there are no roads, and angling pressure is limited. But perhaps a more plausible explanation is that whitefish, tulibees, and other high-fat forage fish thrive in cold water. To grow big, northern pike need a high-fat diet. In the south, whitefish swim at depths that are too oxygen-deficient to support large populations of hungry northerns. Up north, where the water never warms up, the shallows contain abundant schools of whitefish, and the result is an abundance of hog-fat northern pike.

In Manitoba, a top-notch place to catch large northern pike is Big Sand Lake Lodge. In Saskatchewan, a good choice is Hatchet Lake Lodge. Like Plummer's Lodges, Halley's Camps, and other family-run operations, Hatchet Lodge is inseparable from its founder, George Fleming. Three decades ago, long before Hatchet Lake Lodge was featured in

Biggest Fish at Hatchet Lodge	
Northern Pike	35 pounds
Lake Trout	44 pounds
Grayling	4½ pounds

Hatchet Lake Lodge

Field & Stream, *In Fisherman*, *Sports Afield* and in many other outdoor magazines and TV shows, there wasn't much at Hatchet Lake except wind-swept black spruce forests and sand eskers. Around that time a young Scottish man named George Fleming, following the example of hundreds of other Scotsmen before him, arrived from Scotland to work for the Hudson's Bay Company.

After working three straight years as an HBC fur trader without a day off, Fleming purchased a rough shack on an unknown lake in northern Saskatchewan. The fishing was fabulous and Fleming seized upon an idea. A fishing lodge! There were no roads or airstrips in the area, and shipping heavy materials by float plane was too expensive. But Fleming couldn't forget the idea. Not appreciating the enormity of the task ahead, he single-handedly blazed a winter road 40 miles through the bush, at temperatures that sometimes reached 60 below. Ploughing through swamps, forests, and across frozen rivers, he brought in heavy equipment and built a 5000-foot airstrip to provide a link with the outside world. It's much cheaper transporting goods by large, wheeled aircraft than in small float planes, and the airstrip gave him a crucial foothold in the wilderness. Soon, in came the appliances, fuel, outboard motors, and other necessities for the newly-created Hatchet Lake Lodge.

George Fleming

After 25 years of accommodating anglers, Hatchet Lodge is now one of the top fly-in fishing camps in the north. Fleming insists that he's been "lucky," but it's obvious that none of it would have happened without his own brand of stubborn Scottish resolve. Nowadays, guests

“With all the places to fish in Canada, there are few places I’d go back to twice. However, Hatchet Lodges is different, special, terrific, and that’s why we looked forward again to this trip.” —Babe Winkelman “Good Fishing” TV Show

fly from Minneapolis or Winnipeg in a twin-engine Fokker jet aircraft, which travels the 1100 miles to the lodge in a relatively brief four hours. Travelling to most northern lodges often means a long series of plane changes, airport layovers, and tail-end trips on float planes, which are restricted by the whims of the weather. Getting rained in or snowed in has caused many an angler to miss a scheduled aircraft connection in the States, and that can get a little nerve-wracking and expensive. At Hatchet Lodge, guests travel on large, comfortable, instrument-equipped aircraft that land and take off right beside the camp.

The main lodge is a rustic three-storey log structure with a meeting room that will accommodate 30 to 40 friends or convention participants. Guests stay in individual hand-made log cabins with two bedrooms, electricity, carpeted floors, wood stove, and, this is rare, a private bathroom and shower for each bedroom. The day begins with a tray of hot coffee delivered to the front door of your cabin at 6:30 a.m. Half an hour later, the weird skirl of Fleming’s bagpipes summons guests to breakfast in the main lodge. Hatchet Lodge uses only veteran guides and two guests are assigned to each boat. Most of the staff are local Cree people.

In the north, pike tend to hit just about anything that looks like a meal, but anglers won’t go wrong by using flashy spoons designed to imitate a plump baitfish. Once the spawn is over, and the chilly sub-arctic water begins to warm up in the June sun, Hatchet Lake northern pike embark on a virtual feeding frenzy. It’s not unusual for a huge pike to slash voraciously at a spoon five or six times before finally seizing it at boatside and taking off with a wild swipe of the tail that soaks everyone on the boat.

On average, an angler might catch 50 to 75 of these cold-water crocodiles per day – and let most of them go. Fleming and his guides adhere to the catch-and-release policies pursued by all responsible lodge owners in the contemporary north. With the exception of a few fresh fish for lunch – shore lunch, cooked over a fire with all the trimmings – all fish are carefully released. A big pike might be as old as you are. And if you happen to have a ten-year-old along on the trip, you can comfort yourself that catch-and-release fishing will ensure that northern Canada will still have lots of monster fish when that youngster grows up, and takes her own youngsters fishing.

Hatchet is a large lake (18 miles long, 10 miles wide) with more ideal pike habitat than an angler could explore in a full summer. Nevertheless, anglers who are interested in exploring further can travel to 14 nearby fly-out lakes, where walleye, trout, and grayling are abundant. At the end of the fishing day (5:00 p.m.) guests return to the lodge, clean up, have a drink, shoot some bull, and sit down in the dining-room by 7:00 p.m. for a gourmet meal. After a long day on the water, there's nothing like a big plate of prime rib, baked ham, roast turkey, or ribeye steak, chased by a delicious home-baked pie. Then it's off to bed, perchance to dream about another day of catching giant northerns.

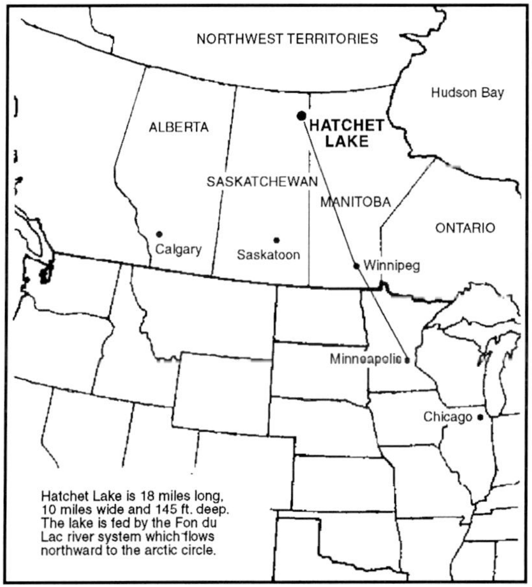

Hatchet Lake is 18 miles long, 10 miles wide and 145 ft. deep. The lake is fed by the Fon du Lac river system which flows northward to the arctic circle.

Hatchet Lake Lodge Ltd.
Box 611, Postal Station G
Calgary, Alberta, Canada T3A 2G5
Winter (Oct.–May.): 403-286-2717
Summer (June–Sept.): 306-633-2132
Toll Free U.S.A.: 1-800-661-9183
Fax: 403-286-7256

BIG SAND, BIG SNAKES

Manitoba is a tall and narrow province with the capital city, Winnipeg, situated close to the American border. Flying north of Winnipeg, a plane barely levels out before entering the northern forest.

For 600 miles, the scene below becomes increasingly desolate, splattered with hundreds of rivers and lakes. Sadly, most of the pristine-looking waterways have been harnessed for hydroelectric power, and it's necessary to fly almost to the roof of Manitoba before finding a truly untouched river, the Seal.

The Seal River winds through an immense region of sandy ridges called "eskers" before emptying into Hudson Bay. There are great opportunities for fishing at the mouth of the Seal, with char, grayling, and yard-long northern pike in abundance, but a lack of comfortable lodging discourages most anglers. In addition, roving polar bears make life interesting for those who fly in and stay in tent camps.

Upstream 100 miles, Tadoule Lake is the ancestral home of the

Big Sand Lake Lodge

WHAT HAPPENED TO THE FOLLOWING ANGLERS WHEN THEY WENT TO BIG SAND LAKE LODGE?

Ed Dubois (WI), Frank Daddona (PA), Kim Richards (MN), Robert Liebig (MN), Matthew Liebig(MN), Larry Haak (IL), Sam Hutton (KS), Mark Hutton (KS), Tom Assalley (IL), Don Daddonna Jr. (PA), Mike Wilcox (MI), Bill Rivas (VA), Harry Chambers (TX), Charles Williams (TN), Bill Townsend (KS), Mark Johnson (MN), Paul Fisher (IA)

ANSWER:

They each caught at least five northern pike weighing over 20 pounds.

Chipewyan people, who still rely on caribou for most of their food. Farther upstream, you can find the only available lodge on the Seal. In the last few years, Big Sand Lake Lodge has quickly become one of the top angling destinations in northern Manitoba.

Big Sand Lake Lodge is owned by a local Cree community and managed by a grizzly-bearded and somewhat legendary woodsman named Trapper Don McCrea. The lodge is an impressive structure built of local logs and boasts a sauna, a hot tub, and a dining room that serves gourmet meals. But it's the staff that makes Big Sand exceptional.

"When we first started up, everybody said that we would never make it," says McCrea. "And frankly, when a guest sees his guide holding a spinning reel upside down, he has a right to wonder."

McCrea points out, though, that the lodge's native guides lived for centuries off the local fish, using nets instead of fishing rods. "Angling is not part of their tradition. But we're really talking about a difference in methodology, not fishing talent."

McCrea held a series of training programs, tackle seminars, and lectures by professional anglers on Fish Finders and structure fishing (using Fish Finders to track the bottom), and soon his guides' aboriginal skills began to take over.

"We caught a few pike the first year," he says. "Nothing exceptional. But anything to do with hunting and fishing, these guys have latent abilities that are way above average. This last season, we caught 500 northern pike over 20 pounds and more than a dozen over 30 pounds. We had one little kid who caught eight pike over 20 pounds. And as far as I'm concerned, most of the credit belongs to the guides."

Big Sand is a catch-and-release lodge. No fish are kept except the walleyes that are selected for shore lunch. Each boat is equipped with a Polaroid camera to record catches of trophies. "We have a 'bragging board' back at the lodge," says McCrea, "and it's become a really popular part of the Big Sand experience. The guests have really gotten into the spirit of catch- and-release. And one thing they all do, getting into the boat in the morning, is check to make sure the camera is all loaded and ready to go. They want a picture up on that bragging board at the end of the day."

Along with the fabulous fishing, there's an abundance of wildlife, some of which can be seen right on the lodge property. Last year, the native waitressess in the dining room had a nightly ritual of feeding a timber wolf, which would saunter out of the woods and walk right up while they scraped the plates. "Oh that damn thing," grumbles McCrea, shaking his head. "That wolf was a big hit with the guests, but I felt like shooting him after about the third time he ran off with my underwear."

McCrea has begun to run expeditions down the Seal River, using jet boats that only draw a few inches of water. The boats are big, comfortable, and safe, but the ride is a wild adventure all the same. In pools below the rapids, the guide holds the boat in the back eddy while the guest works the pool. At one site, the first cast produced a grayling. In 15 minutes, successive casts accounted for a sturdy 3-pound walleye, another grayling, and a 16-pound pike. All went back into the water except the walleye, which made a delicious shore lunch.

Big Sand Lake Lodge
1-1808 Wellington Ave.
Winnipeg, Manitoba R3H 0G3
Phone: 204-774-6666/786-4801 ext. 7942
Fax: 204-774-5500

Walleye

WALLEYE

Scientists call them *Stizostedion vitreum.* But in some parts of northern Canada they're better known as "yellows," and are considered not so much a gamefish as a food stuff like flour or pork.

In eastern Canada, French-speaking anglers call them "doré," in reference to their golden scales. In Ontario and Manitoba, many resident anglers call them pickerel, and seem to feel that referring to this fish by any other name is downright un-Canadian. But biologists, professional anglers, tourist operators, and most serious students of this fish call them walleye and that's the name that has gradually won out.

Under any alias, the walleye is one of the most sought-after gamefish in North America. It's a dogged fighter, and there's no better fish in the frying pan. Found in lakes and rivers from the Arctic to the American south, walleye reach a good average size (2 to 5 pounds), and adapt well to a variety of habitats. Walleye spawn in the spring when the water reaches a temperature of 45 to 50°F. In river mouths, in bays, and along reefs where there is rock rubble or gravel on the bottom, the female walleye lays her eggs, and these are fertilized shortly afterwards by the male. Large walleyes are invariably female and since these large specimens are the most productive and less savoury in the frying pan, they should be released when caught by anglers.

If water levels are stable, some of these eggs

(about ten percent) hatch after about 15 days. Newly hatched walleyes live for a while on their egg sac, then they begin feeding on tiny animals called zooplankton. After reaching 2 inches in length, these miniature walleyes move out into deep water, where they begin to hunt minnows. One walleye egg in 10,000 will actually survive to the end of its first summer, when it will be a fish about 8 inches long. By the time it reaches its second birthday, the walleye's chances of survival will be much improved. Like many predators, it will find itself suddenly in a reversed relationship with all the perch, water beetles, crayfish and other predators that once posed a threat to its survival. Now about 15 to 16 inches long, the walleye will be a little over a pound in weight, and will be on its way to an active life. An 18-inch walleye, at 2 pounds, will have few enemies beyond anglers, and from that point on, the fish will gain half a pound with each inch it grows.

Generally, walleye can be found in shallow water during the post-spawn period (late May) and they migrate gradually into deeper water as the water warms up. By late June, they are established in their summer habitat, and anglers look for walleye around reefs, islands, deep-water weedbeds (20 to 30 feet down), narrow channels between islands, and underwater humps. The best structure for walleye offers deep water (50 feet and deeper) for midday shelter, with a gradual slope leading to shallow flats or weedbeds, where walleye can hunt perch and other forage fish at night.

A basic primer for walleye fishing includes the following points:

1. **Walleye travel in schools.** An angler who catches one should persist in that area, because more walleye are usually nearby. It pays to vary presentation and bait if fishing tapers off. Other fish are probably present, and they may be fussy about accepting one particular lure.
2. **Walleye are usually on, or close to, the bottom.** Bait anglers should check their line regularly to ensure that their bait is just touching the bottom or a few inches above it. Anglers trolling for walleye should feel their lure bumping the bottom regularly. If a walleye is caught in 23 feet of water, it's very likely that most of the school are resting on the structure at that depth. Not 24 feet, not 22, but at that exact contour line along the reef. Often, when one boat catches more fish than another close by, the lucky angler is being more precise about delivering his lure to within striking distance of resting fish.

3. **Walleye eat fish almost exclusively,** so anglers can't go wrong with presenting lures that closely resemble baitfish. "Crankbaits" like the Rapala are good traditional walleye lures. Most of these lures can be fished at any depth, according to whether the walleye are in deep or shallow water.
4. **A slow presentation usually catches walleye more effectively than a quick one.** Walleye are slow, deliberate feeders, particularly since they are usually dormant in daylight hours, so anglers should work their bait gently across the bottom.
5. **Radio-tagged walleyes have demonstrated that this species has two peak feeding hours:** one just after dark, and another that begins about 3 a.m. and lasts until daylight. Scientific studies of radio-tagged walleyes have verified what walleye anglers have long suspected: the marble eyes in a walleye's head are designed for a nocturnal life.

Daytime walleye can be coaxed into biting but the brighter the day, the slower the walleye fishing. Wind, overcast, and the onset of dusk all serve to diminish sunlight penetration into the water, and anything that diminishes sunlight helps put the walleye in a more favourable mood for feeding. Weeds also provide walleye with shelter from the sun, and in recent years anglers have discovered that some walleyes inhabit thick beds of pondweed and coontail all summer long.

Hot dog stands, waterslide parks, and muddy riverbanks might seem like an improbable backdrop for top-notch walleye fishing. But Manitoba's lazy, coffee-brown Red River has the largest walleyes in western Canada. The Red River produces over 200 recorded walleyes annually in the 8 to 13 pound range, and some exceed 15 pounds.

All these from a shallow, muddy river about the width of an interstate highway. The best time to fish the Red is September to October.

For more information, see the Appendix.

Rapala Lure

Rapala Fishing Lures

Manufactured in Finland, Rapala fishing lures are exported to more than 130 countries. There are over 300 types of Rapala available, but several models far outperform the others.

The Shad Rap, for example, quickly became a "must have" for anglers when it was first introduced. Tackle store owners rented them for $20 per day with a $20 deposit and black marketeers sold them for $45. After an article appeared in *Life* magazine in 1962, the little company received orders for three million lures. And Rapala now sells about five million lures annually. To make a long story short, the Rapala is the most successful fishing lure in history.

How did it all happen? In this case, the success of the Rapala illustrates the truth of the old maxim: "Do good work and lots of it." Lauri Saarinen was born in 1905 in Finland, to a family so poor that they lived in a cave. Homeless and anonymous, the family was given the name of the village from which they came, Rapala, a Finnish word meaning mud. Unable to attend school, Lauri Rapala went straight to work as soon as he was big enough to heft an axe. In the summertime he fished, trolling on Lake Paijanne with a line baited with a thousand hooks, and he sold the pike and whitefish he caught to the village market.

Bait, however, was expensive. So Lauri Rapala began experimenting with homemade lures, carving artificial fish from wood and bark, then covering them with tin foil he salvaged from cheese packages. Rapala spent several years designing his lure, and rejected hundreds of models before he settled on an effective floating-diving design that fish loved.

One of his biggest supporters was his wife Elma, who was busy raising their six kids, making saleable handicrafts and managing the fish marketing. She was relieved that she no longer had to lug heavy bait buckets to Lauri, who fished 20 miles away. The new lure was so effective that Rapala challenged some soldiers to a little competition. He used his lure. They used dynamite. After two hours, Rapala returned with 78 pike, and won the contest.

Rapala set up shop, hand-carving the wooden lures, and sold them to vacationers to Lake Paijanne. There's a Finnish community living around Duluth, Minnesota, and the lures began to filter over to America via this cultural pipeline. Word of the lure's effectiveness spread, and in 1962 *Life* magazine ran a story about the Rapala lure. It appeared in the issue featuring a cover story on Marilyn Monroe, right after her death. This was the best-selling *Life* of all time and the publicity resulted in an avalanche of orders for Rapalas. Lauri Rapala was still too poor to respond effectively to such an enormous order, so he went into partnership with an American named Ron Weber. Together, they built a factory and began mass-producing Rapalas. But Rapala himself insisted on maintaining rigid quality standards. Each lure was trolled in a tank and examined by the inventor himself, to make sure it performed like the original.

Weight Calculation for Walleye

(use inches and pounds)

$$\frac{\text{length} \times \text{length} \times \text{length}}{2700} = \text{weight}$$

WALLEYE FACTS

In all varieties of walleye habitat, perch are the number one forage fish. Perch have poor night vision, and walleye catch them easily in darkness. But at different times of the year, walleye focus on other foods. Anglers should know the life cycle of the lake they're visiting, and select lures according to the current hatch.

After half a century of hard labour, Rapala attained fame and wealth. He was honored by the President of Finland, visited by Prince Philip and widely regarded as a hero in his homeland. But Rapala was unimpressed with all his millions of dollars. He lived in a simple house with Elma and his entire life revolved, as always, around the duties of work and family. In 1965 his son Kauko, the baby of the family, went out to test the new Countdown Rapala which would later catch the biggest muskie on record in Canada. His motorboat hit a log boom and he drowned. Lauri Rapala was devasted by the death of his son, and he seemed to lose interest in the lure company and his own life. When he died a few years later, there was only $27,000 in his bank account. He'd given it all to the poor.

Today, Ron Weber's Duluth company, Normark Inc., imports Rapala lures and sells them to anglers of all stripes. Walleye anglers like the Shad Rap and the Countdown Rapala. But the best-selling model of all time is the black-and-silver floating Rapala, the same lure that Lauri Rapala invented to feed his family.

KNOTS FOR WALLEYE FISHING

Modern walleye anglers generally use monofilament line. Walleye will shy away from clutter, swivels, and other terminal gear attached to the line, so expert anglers keep the line and knots simple and clean. To get an edge in walleye fishing, start off with as light a line as you can. Six-pound test line should be sufficient for most conditions.

There are many knots that are strong, clean, and easy to tie, but not so many that work well on slippery monofilament line. A good walleye knot should have a minimum of 90% breaking strength, should be slip-proof, and simple enough that an angler back-trolling into 2-foot waves on a bitterly cold day in October can balance his ham sandwich on one knee and tie it in a couple of seconds.

The **improved clinch knot** is the simplest and most effective way to attach light monofilament line to a ringed-eye hook, such as walleye anglers often use. The angler should be careful to form at least *five* twists in the line before tying the knot. Any less, and the knot will come apart, usually at the worst possible moment.

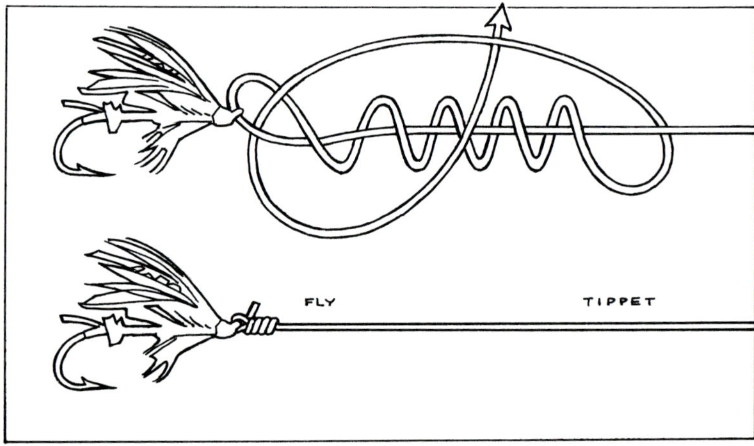

Improved Clinch Knot

FLY FISHING FOR WALLEYE?

The most overlooked walleye lure is the mayfly imitation. In early summer for several weeks mayfly larvae constitute about 70% of a walleye's diet. Mayflies hatch from a mud bottom and undergo a nymph stage, in which they resemble a tiny, fork-tailed minnow. To catch walleye during mayfly season, look for a quiet bay with mature mayfly insects floating on the water. Evening is best.

Using a split shot, a small spinner blade, a tiny hook, and a tidbit of worm (about ½″), slowly troll the shallows and weed edges. This setup imitates a hatching mayfly.

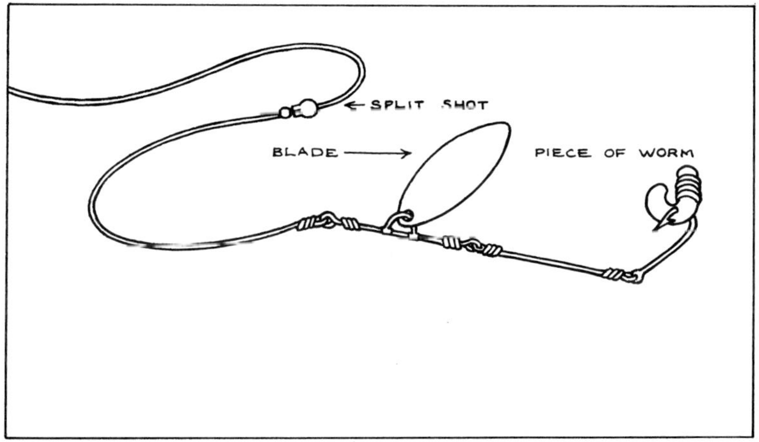

Mayfly Imitation Walleye Lure

As GOOD as it GETS

by Doug Stange

No one is better qualified to review walleye lodges than Doug Stange, Editor of *In Fisherman* magazine. Here is Doug Stange, talking about one of his favorite Canadian fishing holes.

"How good can good get?" I remember thinking. Hours before, I'd shot the biggest bear of my life, a record-book bear for bow-and-arrow, a bear that would provide many fine meals during the coming year. The quarter-ton of animal had taken three of us until midnight to drag into camp. Whew!

A shower later – 1:00 a.m. – a quiet nightcap and dinner at the lodge included a ribeye steak so tender you could cut it with a fork, a good vintage Cabernet Sauvignon, and veggies au gratin. First night in camp, no less.

Now, 5 hours later, sun nipping over the horizon, mist oozing from the lake, I was about to release a lake trout of at least 15 pounds – on my first pass along a shoal not 10 minutes from camp. Time to pour a cup of coffee and slow down. Time to wonder how a world so full of deadlines and disasters could suddenly seem so far away.

Aikens Lodge (photo courtesy Dan D. Gapen Sr.)

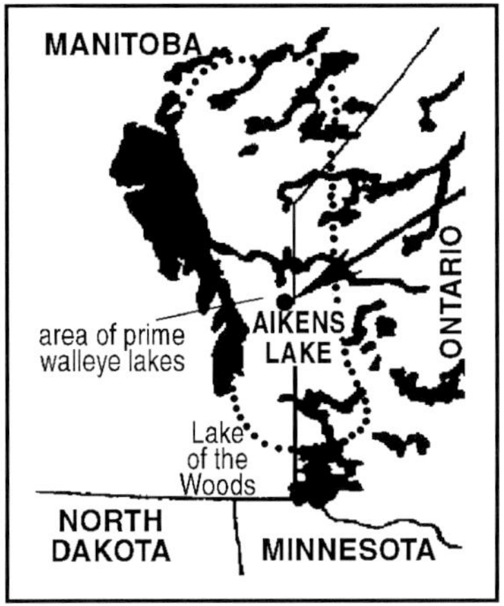

"If we had to pick one area of premium walleye fishing, it would have to be the area shown. Most of these lakes are chockfull of walleyes, many of them large."
—Doug Stange

"Aikens Lake is the place!" Gerry Turenne had told me. I know Gerry from his days working for Travel Manitoba, the Manitoba Tourism department. Today Gerry is the manager of Aikens Lake Wilderness Lodge.

I'd told him my prerogatives for a trip: "Gotta be remote, but easy to get to – don't have much time. Wanna hunt black bear – my one combination hunting and fishing trip of the year. I want walleye, lake trout, and pike. I don't expect to score a trophy of each species, but I want the opportunity – big fish water! And it must be a place readers can afford. But don't tell me about cut-rate food and lodging. Eating well is my hobby. Readers deserve first-class."

"Aikens is the place," he'd said again confidently. After being there I agree. But there's more . . .

Fishing

Lake trout over 30 pounds, walleye over 13 pounds, and pike over 25 pounds are caught each season. While many fly-in lakes offer these three species in combination, not many offer the combined potential of trophies of each species. Fish that large aren't easy, however. Trout commonly run to 12 pounds, walleye to 5 or 6, and pike, to well . . . the best fishing for a huge pike is in May or early June and again in fall. During summer, pike run to about 12 pounds.

Your accommodations include a boat and motor, and a lake map. The lake and connecting rivers are easy to fish. Lake trout are shallow into early June, then head into deeper water during summer. Walleye run rivers during May and June, then frequent rock reefs or weedbeds in bays during summer. Big pike use shallow seedbeds during early summer. Pike to 12 pounds live in weeds all summer.

Guides are available if you want help finding fish. A tackle shop is located on site, too. Plus a fish cleaning room and a fish cleaning and freezing service. Aikens, however, stresses catch-and-release of big fish. You can have a trophy of each species and enough smaller fish to enjoy upon returning home. Smaller fish are kept for shore lunches.

Food and lodging

Comfortable cabins and fantastic food. This is as good as it gets, especially the food. Start the day with coffee delivered to your door. Each meal is prepared with flair, and you won't go away hungry.

Meals are served in the rustic, beautiful and functional lodge. A game room includes a bar and pool tables as well as the latest video games.

I could go on and on . . . and on. Add beautiful beaches to Aikens' long list of pluses. The perfect choice for a family trip. Aikens is located just northeast of Winnipeg, Manitoba in the Atikaki Provincial Park. Fly-out options are available too, but why don't you find out for yourself?

Aikens Lake Wilderness Lodge
Box 98, St. Boniface P.O.
Winnipeg, Manitoba   R2H 3H1
Phone or Fax: 204-237-LAKE

WOLVES & WALLEYES

A gang of us were staying in a cabin on the English River, taking part in what Halley's Camps Incorporated calls a "Winter Adventure Vacation." Northwestern Ontario has some of the best walleye fishing in Canada. But until recently, everyone restricted their walleye fishing to summertime. Gene Halley is trying to persuade people that they're missing something – winter walleye.

Around midnight, after Sally and the others had gone to bed, Gene decided that he and I should go outside and try calling some wolves. We were feeling inspired after a good supper, some stories, some whisky, and Gene had a cigarette drooping from the corner of his mouth as we stepped out into the crackling winter darkness.

Overhead, the sky blazed with *aurora borealis*, green and pink ribbons that flamed above the spruce tops, faded, then exploded brilliantly in some other reach of the sky.

Preparing for his performance, Gene took a pull on his cigarette and spat on the snow. Despite the 30°F air temperature, he wore only a wool undershirt. As the 33-year-old co-owner of Halley's Camps, Gene Halley has flown bush planes through more storms, argued with more bears, and fallen through more holes in the ice than he can remember. He doesn't, in other

Halley's Camp Interior

words, have to act tough. He is. After flipping his smoke in a twinkling end-over-end into the snow he stood for a few moments with his thumbs hooked in his pockets, silent. Was he trying to get in touch with the wolves telepathically? Finally he cupped his hands over his mouth and breathed in.

A wild sound poured out. "AR-ROOOOOOOO-O-O-O."

We waited. But there was only the utter silence of winter. Night. The sense of one's own heart working. Thump. Thump. The stars.

Gene howled again. Silence. "I thought I heard one," he said.

I didn't.

"You try it," he said.

I attempted a sick howl. Gene was polite enough not to say anything. "Sounds like I stubbed my toe," I said.

"Use your gut," he whispered, patting his belt buckle. "Push the sound out from way down here."

I tried it again. Gene sang out like an air raid siren, a wild rising call that made the northern lights step back. His howls had a sad fade at the end, not so much hunting songs as laments. He cocked his head and listened. "Did you hear that?"

"No."

"I heard something."

"Probably the girls swearing at us for waking them up."

We howled and waited, howled and waited. The frigid air was starting to knife through the pleasant insulation of our late-night whisky. "They'll probably come skulking around the cabin after we go to bed," Gene said. "To see what we're up to."

Ice Safety Rules for Winter Walleye Fishing

- Ice is thinner in the middle of the lake than along the edges. Drive close to shore.
- River ice varies continuously in thickness. Current means danger.
- Thick snow means thin ice.
- Sudden application of brakes in a vehicle shifts weight forward, and may crack ice.

Maximum Safe Loads on Ice

2 inches	1 person
3½ inches	snow machine
8 inches	automobile
12 inches	3 ton truck
26 inches	loaded tractor trailer

Now come on, Gene, I thought. You don't have to give me the tourist stuff.

But the next morning, I saw that he was right. Gene often says things which turn out to be right. After a big breakfast of bacon and eggs we packed up to go ice fishing. Outside, the sun sparkled on the snow. We fired the Arctic Cats to life, and stamped our feet, buttoned our hoods. Bait, coffee, sandwiches, and drinks were strapped onto the back of Gene's snow machine, tucked into a cooler to keep them warm. Cruising downhill, we saw them – a fresh necklace of wolf tracks in the snow. "Look at that," Gene said. "They came. Five of them."

All day long I thought about our visitors. There's no creature that better embodies the elusive quality of wilderness than the timber wolf, and just seeing those large, splayed footprints in the snow by the cabin was a thrill for me. But wolves were my own fetish. There's more to do at Halley's Camps than look at footprints and howl at the moon. Gene and his family preside over an area of wilderness that's several thousand kilometres in area, and with one of their fully winterized, remote cabins as a home base you can ski, sketch cliffs and jackpines, hunt for Indian rock paintings, photograph moose, caribou, ravens, foxes, wolves, and the other creatures that live in the area. Best of all, you can fish. Halley's Camps has access to an incredible variety of lakes. Muskie, lake trout, smallmouth bass, walleye, and huge northern pike are all active in the wintertime, and just waiting for someone to bore a hole through the ice and deliver a snack.

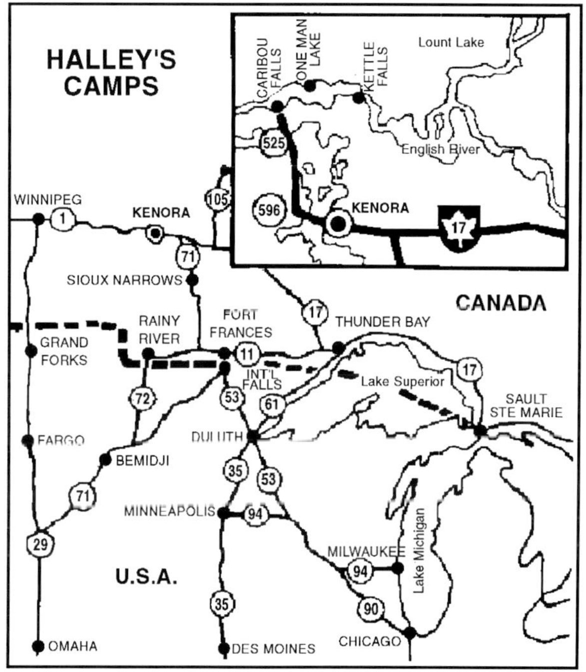

Halley's Camp is located four hours northeast of Winnipeg on Ontario Highway 596. From the base camp, groups travel by snow machine to winterized outpost cabins. Guides, food, and equipment are included in all package prices. For brochures and information call Gene or Wanda Halley at 1-807-224-4536.

From our base camp at One Man Lake, we snowmobiled across the ice, over a wooded hill, and across another lake. The low rising sun flooded a scene of incredible beauty. Big feathery pines silvered with frost, wind-rippled snowboard scalloped with blue shadow. We saw wildlife, and signs of wildlife, around every corner. A lone red fox watched us from the shoreline. Moose, deer, and wolf tracks were everywhere. By one island, we saw the signs that a pack of five wolves had tackled a deer last night. A few scruffs of hair, some trampled snow, and drops of blood told the story. In this chapter, the deer won. His tracks led up to the woods. The wolves, shrugging, went off in search of a less rambunctious animal.

At a lake with no name we drilled some holes in the ice. Gene went to shore and built a crackling fire. Made some coffee. Before he rejoined us, we already had two fat walleyes on the ice and we'd caught and released a 36-inch northern pike. Gene walked over and nodded when he saw the fish. "While you've been goofing off," I said, "we've been working. And we released a nice big spottie." So the morning went. Lots of fish. A few eating-size walleyes, to their misfortune, were kept for dinner. And what a gorgeous, mild winter day. The sun beat down. We were getting a tan. "I've got another one," somebody said, cranking another walleye onto the ice. "You shoulda been here last week," Gene said. "When the fishing was good."

That night Gene went home for a quick visit to his family. His snowmobile gave a panther scream as he took off into the darkness. It took our group several hours to cover the 30-kilometre trail up from the main lodge to the winter cabin. But Gene, with his Mackenzie brothers toque pulled low on his eyes, would cover that same distance in 20 minutes. We ate a delicious supper in his absence, then washed the dishes and listened to CBC's "Ideas." The weather report called for another night of plunging temperature. Back in the city, I thought, people would be cursing and complaining. Here, the cold was an adventure.

Sally and I went outside to look at the northern lights. The snow was frozen and hard. We walked quietly, and stood by the lake. Banners of green and pink ribboned overhead, everything so quiet we felt compelled to whisper. "Gene showed me how to howl like a wolf," I said. "Do you want me to show you?"

She nodded.

I demonstrated one of my sick wolf howls. We listened. No answer. "You try it."

She attempted a feeble whoop, almost as bad as my own

"Drive it from down here."

"I feel silly."

"Pretend you're lonesome for your big lobo."

Another howl, better this time, and I joined her to give a stereo effect. Almost immediately an answer came from across the lake. First one low, moaning cry, then a rising series of whoops that combined with others far away. Distant echoes rolled back and forth across the lake, then lifted, then faded. Timber wolves!

I can't believe this, I thought. Wait until Gene gets back. Sally sent another howl into the air and the wolves across the lake answered. Then I replied. For five minutes we howled back and forth. First the wolves. Then us. Then all together, our voices rising in a wild, midnight choir.

Muskellunge

MUSKELLUNGE

Esox masquinongy operates under about 50 other names, including muskie, lunge, blue pike, and tiger muskie. It is officially described under Canadian law as the "Maskinonge," a name derived from the Ojibway people. In their language, "mass" means ugly and "kinonge" means fish.

The muskellunge is generally larger than the northern pike and exhibits different behaviour and feeding patterns. Close up, a muskellunge is generally silver, whereas the pike is green with bean-shaped yellow marks along its sides. Along its lower jaw, the muskie has six to nine sensory pores, whereas the pike has only five.

When they are seen at a distance, however, under a dock or following a lure, it's not quite as easy to differentiate a muskie from a large northern pike. After some practice, experienced anglers can see a large shadow in the water and tell whether it's a pike or muskie. Muskie move quickly, with self-confidence, and show little fear of boats. A pike's head, seen from above, is U-shaped. A muskie's face is sharper, a spade rather than a shovel. But overall, recognizing a muskie at a distance is a gut feeling. For example, a muskie will sometimes boil on the surface when a boat pulls up. It's hard to imagine such a display of territorial aggression from a northern pike.

Esox masquinongy was once a saltwater fish, and is believed to have entered North America

Muskie require deep cold-water lakes to grow to a large size. Only deep lakes that support a good population of quality baitfish (like ciscoes and whitefish) will support large muskies. Ontario has the best muskie fishery in North America. But of Ontario's 250,000 water bodies, only 200 contain muskie. Fewer still contain muskies of significant size.

via the Mississippi River. Fossil muskies have been dug up from Pleistocene deposits in Oklahoma, and from Tertiary deposits in Europe so muskellunge literally travelled around the world. The retreat of glaciers about 10,000 years ago reversed the flow of many rivers and left this great fish stranded in the freshwater basins of the north. In northern lakes and rivers, muskellunge are late spawners. In fact, the muskie is usually the last fish to spawn in the spring, well after the pike and walleye. In weedy bays and along sand beaches, enormous female muskies can often be seen swimming in very shallow water in late May, accompanied by a pair of smaller males. Characteristically, they display little fear of boats, and an observer in a canoe can come quite close. The angling season for muskie does not open until after the spawning season in mid-June and it is properly illegal to pester spawning fish with lures during the spawn.

Pike, walleye, and perch hatch before muskie, so all these fingerlings, which will soon learn to live in fear of the muskie's shadow, enjoy a brief grace period during which they can feed on tiny muskies. But muskellunge grow quickly, and by their second birthday they are about 15 inches long, big enough to turn the tables on perch, bass, and other predators. It takes about 5 to 7 pounds of forage fish beyond a maintenance diet to make one pound of muskellunge, and by the time the muskie is 4 years old, it will be about 31 inches long and weigh about 8 pounds. At this point, the muskellunge no longer has any natural enemies except humans.

Muskie fishing is a sport for purists. The old cliché that "it takes 10,000 casts to catch a muskie" has some truth to it. Muskie occupy the very top of the food pyramid, so they are less numerous than the critters beneath them. To get a meeting with a muskie can take some doing. And most anglers would rather dunk a minnow and try to catch a few walleye for dinner, than fish day after day with nothing to show but a sore arm. To further discourage the less-than-fanatic angler, it's becoming an unspoken rule of muskie fishing that, after those 10,000 casts, any muskellunge that ends up on the end of your line should be carefully released. In the old days, an angler might win admiration by dragging a big muskellunge onto the marina dock, but nowadays that's the fastest way to earn a few rolled eyeballs and muttered comments. In this day and age of taxidermist's reproductions, an angler can take a picture of a fish and wind up with a mount that looks as good as, or better than, the traditional stuffed fish. So there's simply no reason to kill a big muskellunge.

Muskie fishing is a long-established and serious pastime. But just because anglers have been throwing lures at muskie for a hundred years, it doesn't mean that they've learned everything there is to know. Biologists like Bernard LeBeau, of the University of Toronto, have recently completed studies that utterly overturn our understanding of muskellunge and how they live.

To test your knowledge of muskellunge, see if you can determine which of the following common beliefs about muskie are true.

True or False?

1. Muskie generally frequent one particular spot, a weedbed, reef, channel or other piece of ideal habitat.
2. Muskellunge feed in shallow water, then move into deep water to rest and digest their meal.
3. They are solitary in pursuing their prey.
4. Muskie feed in the daytime and rest at night.
5. They lie in wait for fish, rather than swimming long distances in search of food.
6. Muskie normally consume a single, large fish then sleep it off for a week or so. When the fish is digested, they become active again.

Answers

All the statements are false.

1. A large muskie hunts throughout a home range that may be over 1000 acres in size. Muskie regularly patrol this home range, and often cover long distances (as much as 14 miles) in short periods of time.
2. Deep water is the primary feeding area of big muskie in the summer. When patrolling this primary feeding area, a large muskie will usually cruise at a depth of about 30 feet. They move to shallow water rest areas (sun-warmed weed flats, etc.) to digest their food.

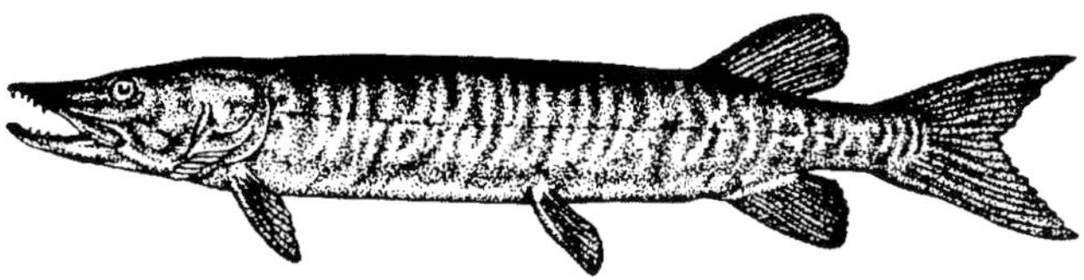

3. Researchers have determined that large muskies commonly cooperate to hunt and herd baitfish. Muskie home ranges commonly overlap, with many muskies sharing prime habitat.
4. Muskie hunt actively at night, as has been proven by numerous anglers in recent years.
5. Big Bertha, one of LeBeau's study fish, travelled 6 miles, moving from a small lake to a larger one. She made this round trip every day, leaving in the morning and returning in the afternoon.
6. The largest muskie caught in the last 25 years was taken on a 4⅜-inch lure. Large muskies commonly feed on ciscoes and small whitefish. The stereotypical notion of a large muskie consuming a 20-inch white sucker, then becoming lethargic for a week, is probably an exception to the rule. Find schools of deep water baitfish, and you've found muskies.

THE BEST KNOT FOR MUSKIE FISHING

Many anglers use braided dacron line for muskie fishing. Others use new high-tech monofilament, believing that it is easier to cast and more resistant to abrasion. In either case, anglers generally use very strong line (in the range of 30 lb. test) under the theory that the real challenge of muskie fishing is not so much out-wrestling the fish, as getting the fish to strike in the first place. From a conservationist point of view, a muskie that breaks the line will swim away with a big wooden jerkbait or bucktail in its jaw, and its survival would be in question. So use strong line, and release the fish afterwards.

Whether using monofilament or dacron, most muskie hunters are happy with the performance of the **Double Improved Clinch Knot**. The double version differs from the improved clinch knot used by walleye anglers in that the angler passes the line **twice** through the hook eye before twisting the line five times, and completing the knot. Passing the line twice disperses stress across two loops of line, and makes the knot slightly more resistant to the inevitable fatigue caused by heavy muskie lures. Even with this knot, anglers should snip off several feet of line and retie their terminal knot every day before going casting.

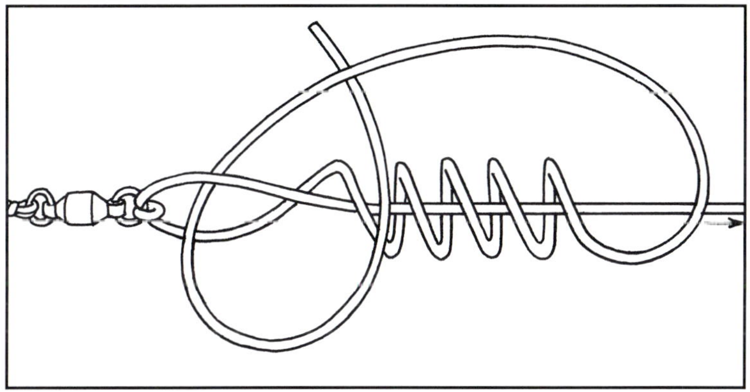

Double Improved Clinch Knot

Wooden Muskie Baits

Canadian fishing lure manufacturers keep their cards pretty close to their chests, so there's some guesswork involved in determining which companies are biggest and most profitable. But unconfirmed industry reports indicate that Canada's largest fishing lure company is the Lucky Strike Bait Works of Peterborough, Ontario.

Back in the 1920s, pattern-makers were the artisans of the woodworking trades, and it was a pattern-maker named Frank Edgar who started the Lucky Strike Bait Works company in 1929. Like many great lure manufacturers, Edgar was a skilled tradesman who was drawn into the business by his love of angling. Edgar believed that true sportsmen always choose artificial lures over live bait. He couldn't afford artificials, because of the Depression, so he began building his own lures. According to his neighbours, Edgar developed the annoying habit of sawing 10 or 15 inches off the handles of any brooms he found unguarded.

These broom handles became the raw material of Lucky Strike's earliest wooden baits. In Edgar's words, "They were awful-looking things," but they caught fish. And as a result, people wanted to buy them. Rumours of Edgar's wooden lures spread to Toronto, where a tackle distributor saw them, liked their

Lucky Strike

action, and ordered 10,000. Frank Edgar did some quick mathematics, and realized he could make more money if he quit his day job. Now after more than 60 years in the business, Lucky Strike has captured about 15% to 20% of the Canadian market. And the company is still owned and operated by the Edgar family, in the persons of Bill, Frank's son, and Mary, the founder's granddaughter.

Weight Conversion Formula for Muskellunge

(use inches and pounds)

$$\frac{\text{length} \times \text{length} \times \text{length}}{3500} = \text{weight}$$

Artificial lures fall into three general categories: spinners, spoons, and plugs. Although the Lucky Strike company started out producing plugs, eventually it diversified into producing spinners and spoons. During the 1950s, wooden lures gradually faded from popularity, replaced by plugs with plastic bodies, and Lucky Strike diversified into manufacturing hundreds of varieties of metal spoons, spinners, and other fishing equipment. Across North America, all the grand old wooden lure companies made similar changes, or disappeared like dinosaurs. Kim Rhodes, grandson-in-law of Frank Edgar, says that wooden lures are simply too labour-intensive to produce. "There have really been no innovations in the manufacturing process since Frank Edgar's day," he says. "It's hard to cut corners and make a good product. Plastic lures have swept the market."

Lucky Strike makes a number of popular and excellent metal lures. The Half Wave spoon, for example, is one of the best trout lures ever designed. But out of sheer stubbornness, the family-owned company continues to make large wooden muskie lures, just like the ones Frank Edgar founded the company with. "We're not making much of a buck from this line," Rhodes says. "We make them too well. Each lure receives a number of coats of sealer and varathane before we even start putting on the paint job. You see, the best wooden lures are completely watertight, because once water gets into a lure you get splitting, dry rot, and the added weight of the water ruins the lure's action."

Lucky Strike concentrates most of its marketing effort in Canada. Muskie fishing is an obsessive hobby, and countless wooden muskie lures are designed, marketed, and sold by hobby-designers around North America. Examples are the Suick, the Hawg Wobbler, and the Bobby Bait. These companies are not as big or as long-established as Lucky Strike. But any wooden lure, in this plastic world, is a valuable article. And once an old muskie plug, battered and scarred by too many run-ins with foul-tempered muskies, is ready for retirement, you don't put it in the garbage with the bubble packages and the rest of the plastic junk. You hang it in a place of dignity, up there above the mantelpiece.

The Amazing Shrinking Muskie

In 1957 a New Yorker named Arthur Lawton caught a 64½-inch muskie in the St. Lawrence River. Lawton claimed that his fish weighed 69 pounds and 15 ounces – a new world record. Until that time, the record was held by Louie Spray, with a 69-pound, 11-ounce fish caught in the Chippewa Flowage. Lawton submitted witness statements and a poor photograph to back up his claim, but because the fish itself never appeared (he cut it up) there were persistent challenges to Lawton's credibility.

Years later, a Wisconsin muskie guide named John Dettloff became annoyed with the innuendo about Lawton's record, so he set out to verify the story once and for all. Instead, Dettloff began to have doubts himself. The famed angler A.J. McClane, on his death bed, left Dettloff an affidavit that he doubted the story, and requested that Dettloff continue his investigation. Dettloff analysed Lawton's photo and took it to some independent legal investigators and a team of photo experts at the University of California. The verdict? The fish in the photo was clearly half a foot shorter than the 64 inches Lawton had claimed.

As a result of Dettloff's work, the International Gaming Fish Association has recently stripped Lawton of the record and given it back to Louie Spray. Too late, however. Spray died in 1984.

Portrait of a MUSKIE MAN

If you go to Minaki, Ontario, and ask people in the local bar for the name of the best hunting and fishing guide within 100 miles, most of them will probably say "Jimmy Anderson." If you tell them that you're a poacher, and you're planning to go out and filch a few beavers on Jimmy's trap line, they'll probably tell you what to expect. "Jimmy will cut a forked stick and hold you under water until the bubbles stop coming up."

Other bar patrons will probably throw in a few stories of their own: about the time that Jimmy tracked a bear through the woods by following the trail of bent twigs as if he was in a Tarzan movie. Or about Jimmy's prowess as the winter carnival's champion arm-wrestler: "Bang. You no sooner take his hand than your knuckles hit the table." Or the time he went swimming in a snowstorm, when a boat drifted away. Climbing out of the lake, he shook off like a grizzly and shrugged in dismissal. "I don't get cold." If, during the telling of these tales, a huge shadow falls across the table, you'd better sit up straight. Because the man himself has arrived.

In person, Jimmy Anderson is a 250-pound Ojibway with a neat black moustache and, always, a brand new pickup truck parked outside. For all the mythic tales about him, he's surprisingly soft-spoken. His characteristic gesture seems to be a dismissive shrug, as if there's nothing very remarkable about going out and catching 45-pound muskies on a regular basis. And it's true that life in the backwoods seems a little easier for Jimmy than for the rest of us. Fishing, hunting, trapping, fighting forest fires, it's all old hat to him.

I met him 20 years ago, when we worked as fishing guides together, and while he always caught more fish than anyone else, the thing I remember is how he shrugged it off. At noon, while the rest of us scurried around, trying to head off the ever-looming disasters of preparing lunch on an open fire, Jimmy would handle his job, someone else's too, and still have time for a running comic monologue with the guests and an endless repertoire of complicated, deadpan jokes. You'd stand up after cleaning the fish, and find out he had tied your belt loop to the tree. You'd go fishing after lunch, reach into the pocket of your jacket, and come out with a walleye head.

Jimmy Anderson (photo: Cheryl Albuquerque)

THE BRYANT CUP

Jimmy Anderson (r) and his muskie fishing partner, the late Glen Tindall.

For the last 14 years a ragtag group of old-time fishing guides, Jimmy Anderson included, has got together for an annual fishing derby called the Bryant Cup Muskie Hunt.

Come August first, several dozen other middle-aged guys who should know better abandon their jobs, homes, and families to head for Minaki, Ontario to join Jimmy and a handful of other men who still work as guides, and spend two weeks doing nothing but fishing for muskellunge.

The Bryant Cup is named after Doug Bryant, an old-time fishing guide from this neck of the woods. I first met Doug 14 years ago, when I worked as a fishing guide and lived in a clapboard bunkhouse near Minaki Lodge called "The Swamp." The Swamp was not a fancy place. The floors were covered with mouldy indoor-outdoor carpeting, which permanently stank of fuel oil. Boots and jeans and jackets were flung haphazardly in every corner.

The tables were littered with tangled fishing lures, beer empties and girlie magazines. But it was an ideal spot for a young man to get an education. Along with the other guides I majored in knife-sharpening, rolling cigarettes, and telling lies. The lies usually featured a starring role for a fabled and elusive fish called the muskie.

The muskie was a fabled fish because none of us had ever seen one. We left Murray's Camp every morning and fished for walleye until noon, had shore lunch, and cast all afternoon, but we never laid eyes on a muskie. We couldn't figure it out. Like most rookie guides, we imagined ourselves to be dashing and skilled young fellows. Frenchie was a tall, moustachioed individual who never tied his bootlaces. Racing his boat against another guide one day, he stuck his finger inside the cowling to push on the throttle and lost his finger on the fly wheel. Browner drove the lodge's pontoon boat, taking vacationers on a tour through the islands and bays of the Winnipeg River system, and frequently had no idea where he was. Red Bob, out with his guests one day, lapsed into a daydream at the helm of his Lund and ran full speed up onto a huge granite reef.

But worst of all, we caught no muskies. The closest any of us came to one of the legendary fish was back at camp, where we gazed up at the snaggle-toothed monster above the fireplace.

We might have lost faith entirely if not for the intercession of a couple of older guides named Johnny Rheault and Doug Bryant. Every night, down at the filleting shack, Johnny and Doug would entertain the naïve younger guides with lurid tales of the olden days. Doug was a big man, with the rolling walk and rounded shoulders of a buffalo. Johnny Rheault was a tough, sharp-eyed little man, with a decal of Mighty Mouse on the door of his pickup. He was an ex-game warden, full of stories, some of them true. He assured us that the muskies were out there, if we had the patience to go after them.

Best Muskie Waters in Ontario

Eagle Lake,
Georgian Bay,
Lac Seul,
Lake of the Woods,
St. Lawrence River,
Winnipeg River

He told us that on a June day in 1947, for example, a guest caught an enormous muskie not half a mile from the front door of the Swamp. Johnny was there when the boat came in. The guest weighed the dead muskie and there was much excitement when everyone realized that the 59-pound fish was a new world record. And Johnny had a healthy enough sense of humour to agree to photograph the happy tourist, with his fish, before arresting him. It was two days before the season opened.

Gary Lovett, better known as Browner, is

WHAT'S SO GREAT ABOUT LUNDS?

If you travel in the back country of the Rocky Mountains, you want to get a sure-footed little cow pony, about 14 hands high, that can sniff its way home in a blizzard or slide rump-first down a mountainside without batting an eye.

If you go fishing in the north country, you want to get a high-transom Lund boat that will speed over three-foot swells or whack an occasional submerged log with the same casual grace as that cow pony. Everywhere you go in the lake country of Canada you see fishing guides driving that same Lund boat and wearing the same baseball hat. It's possible that these guys lack

imagination. But more likely, they know a little bit about fishing boats and they've decided that Lund makes a good product.

What's so great about Lunds? I'm not on their payroll, by the way. For starters, when Lund builds a fishing boat they build them to last. Only heavy-gauge aluminum is used, the seams are double-riveted. The seats are incorporated into the hull, and act as heavy braces for the sides of the boat. A Lund boat, therefore, is as tight as a drum, and that's why it feels "rhino-tough" when you're smacking through wind-tossed waves.

a Hobbit-sized individual with a weathered baseball hat attached jauntily to the side of his head. Browner listened to Doug and Johnny's stories and launched his fellow guides in an all-out effort to catch muskies. "We enlisted Doug and a couple of the older guys," Browner says. "We thought that it would give us credibility. But I guess in those days not even the senior guides knew much about muskies."

Shortly afterwards, Doug Bryant died in a boating accident, and Browner, who had by now appointed himself the derby's Dictator For

---

In addition, anglers like the way these boats are designed. Working 10 hours a day in a fishing boat, week after week, enables one to develop a fine loathing for all those minor annoyances that the designers back at the factory may have overlooked. Seat positioning, for example. How many times have you seen guides sitting up on the splash rail at the rear of the boat because the factory-installed seats are an uncomfortable distance from the motor? How many times have guides and guests had to stumble over fishing rods and frying pans because there's no place to stow loose equipment? And whose bright idea was it to put gas tanks in the rear of the boat, where you already have three or four hundred pounds of engine and guide sitting right on the lowest freeboard in the whole craft?

Lund says their boats are "guide tested." And they're pretty serious about actually listening to what guides have to say. According to Dave Wilson, Director of Marketing for Lund, "We're really good at building a solid hull, one that performs well in the water. But we recognize that people who spend their whole day working on the water probably have some valuable insights on layout and design." So when Lund embarked on a program of building the ultimate fishing camp boat, they contacted one of Ontario's ultimate fishing guides, Jimmy Anderson.

"We get a lot of people with good general suggestions," says Wilson. "But one of our dealers recommended Anderson as a guy who had a lot of very good, specific ideas. We talked with Jimmy and he must have come to the factory about six times to help us design storage compartments, rod lockers, casting deck, and seat layout. The result is the 17-foot Voyageur, which we think is the best camp boat ever made."

Best places to fish for muskies on Eagle Lake

Andy Myers Lodge
General Delivery
Vermilion Bay, ON
P0V 2V0
Ph: 807-227-2610

Eagle Lake Sportsman's Lodge
General Delivery
Vermilion Bay, ON
P0V 2V0
Ph: 807-227-5318

Stanley's West Arm Camp
General Delivery
Vermilion Bay, ON
P0V 2V0
Ph: 807-227-2199

Bear Trail Lodge
General Delivery
Waldhof, ON
P0V 2V0
Ph: 807-227-2625

Life, decided to name the annual competition The Bryant Cup Muskie Hunt. "Doug got the derby named after him because he was the first member to die," Browner explains. "He was a lousy fisherman, but a great sport. He'd go out and fish hard all evening, whether he caught anything or not. He had the true spirit of the hunt."

The tournament is now 15 years old, and Dictator-for-Life Browner has cut the Hunt down to two weeks. But the catch has soared to over 40 fish. And the average size has increased from 10½ pounds in 1979 to 15½ pounds. Jimmy Anderson, of course, wins the hunt with monotonous predictability. Last year, he took "Big Fish" category with a 56-inch long muskie, 33 inches in girth, that he deliberately underestimated, with a characteristic shrug, at 38 pounds. In this particular fish derby, you earn status by down-grading the size of the fish you've caught. Anderson one-ups everyone by regularly insisting his 45-pounders probably only weigh 35 and change. Head Dictator Browner says, "Our muskie population is in very good shape. And the increase is due to the spread of catch-and-release fishing. We don't even encourage our members to lift a big fish out of the water. We tag 'em, tape them, and let them go."

The local muskies, like the Muskie Hunters, have become characters in their own right. Bernice is a well-known big female who lives in the channel near my partner's house in Minaki. Long and slender, Bernice weighed in at 28 pounds when she was first caught 5 years ago. She has only been subdued once since then as far as we know, but, judging from her many sultry appearances, she's alive and well and still growing. If you're casting and you see something following your lure, long and sinuous as an anaconda, don't scream. It's only Bernice.

Old Jingles is another famous local Minaki muskie. Jingles is an enormous beast generally considered large enough to break the world record. Seen at various times by members of the

Hunt, Old Jingles has achieved legendary status. Browner has seen her several times, he says. "She's about 6 feet long," he says. "How many pounds? I don't know. But I'll tell you something. I've played with lots of 40-pounders, and she's twice as big."

Anderson seems to know a lot of individual fish in the system, and he says he saw Jingles last summer. "She followed in three times," he says. "She has sides that are 18 inches high. I'd say she's about 90 pounds, easily a world record."

Even for those who haven't seen her, Jingles haunts the imagination. Huge as a railway tie, scarred, maned with moss and frayed fishing line, the big muskie supposedly wears so many walleye spinners that she jingles like a carriage horse when she crashes out of the water.

To win the Bryant Cup, a team usually has to chalk up six or seven good muskies. The Head Dictator tries to set a good example by sometimes catching as many as nine fish on his own. Jimmy Anderson sets a good example by catching and releasing bigger muskies than most of us have ever seen. The rest of us, however, are not as dedicated and professional.

The cowboy boots, bellbottoms, and long hair we wore at the beginning of the Hunt have been traded in for Hush Puppies, fortrel slacks, and a bald spot. As the guides and ex-guides grow older, nature and fate are beginning to pick off the members of the hunt. This past winter, Jimmy Anderson's muskie derby team partner, Glen Tindall, as handsome and smooth and serious a muskie fisherman as you've ever seen, was killed by a train. Jimmy Anderson himself, recovering from a vicious stroke, is up and walking again and promising to be back on the water again, come summer, driving his big guide-tested and guide-designed Lund Voyageur wide open down the river. Out guiding again.

Maybe this summer he's going to catch Old Jingles.

Good places for muskie anglers on the Lake of the Woods

Crawford's Camp
General Delivery
Sioux Narrows, ON
P0X 1N0
Ph: 808-226-5646

Motlong's Cdn. Camps
General Delivery
Sioux Narrows, ON
P0X 1N0
Ph: 807-226-5240

Totem Lodge
General Delivery
Sioux Narrows, ON
P0X 1N0
Ph: 807-226-5275

Ash Rapids Camp
Box 1090
Kenora, ON
P9X 3X7
Ph: 807-543-4025

Indianhead Lodge
General Delivery
Sioux Narrows, ON
P0X 1N0
Ph: 807-226-5558

The Rod and Reel
General Delivery
Sioux Narrows, ON
P0X 1N0
Ph: 807-226-5240

Yellowbird Lodge
General Delivery
Sioux Narrows, ON
P0X 1N0
Ph: 807-226-5279

Center Island Resort
P.O. Box 36
Oak Island, MN
56741 U.S.
Ph: 807-543-4030

MUSKIES ACCORDING TO JIMMY

"Give me a surface bait like a Hawg Wobbler. I like those surface baits more than anything. But if I'm using a sub-surface bait I like a small one. Don't use big lures. Too many guys use those giant lures. I don't care what the biologists say, I think muskies eat mostly small fish.

"If you meet an aggressive fish, don't bother her. Go away for half an hour and then try her again. If a fish has been caught, it will be at least 2 weeks before she'll come anywhere near a boat again.

"Once you've hooked a muskie, fight it fast and don't make a big deal over it. Keep your rod tip in the water so she won't jump. The worst thing you can do is get that fish all worn out. They'll kill themselves fighting if you let them.

"I always net a fish. If you play them until you can handle them by hand, you've played them too long. I put a towel on her head and talk to her, quiet her down, then get her back in the water as quickly as possible. Then I stay around for ten minutes, to make sure she's gotten away all right."

MINAKI LODGE

For muskie anglers, the fanciest fishing resort on the Winnipeg River is Minaki Lodge. Currently owned and operated by Four Seasons, Minaki Lodge was built by the Canadian National Railway in 1925.

The lodge is constructed entirely of log and stone, and is the second largest log structure in the world. The largest is in Montebello, in Quebec. Inside the main entrance, the visitor is struck by the spaciousness and the grandeur of the place – the 60-foot-high log-buttressed ceiling, black iron chandeliers hanging from heavy chains, stained glass windows, huge moose heads, and a massive stone fireplace in the centre of the hall.

Guests stay in separate wings and meet Jimmy Anderson or one of the other local guides down at the marina dock. Ten minutes' boat ride away from the whispering butlers, jazz piano stylings, and *haute cuisine* of Minaki Lodge, you're out in the wilderness with hundreds of miles of shoreline and muskie habitat to explore. Sometimes it's unnecessary to

Minaki Lodge
Box 26
Minaki, Ontario
P0X 1J0
Ph: 807-224-4000

Minaki Lodge

go long distances, though. Some of the best muskie habitat on the river is right among the wharves, weedbeds, and old sunken crib docks within the town limits. In 1947, a guest caught a world-record muskellunge about 200 feet from the Lodge dock.

Minaki Lodge is not primarily a fishing lodge, and never has been. Launched initially as a spiffy railway hotel, the Lodge has been through a number of incarnations. Conference centre, family resort, grand hotel – the Lodge has had as many identities as owners. But anglers have always stayed there, for both the sumptuous accommodation and the excellent muskie fishing.

With a sporty nine-hole golf course, swimming pool, tennis courts, and assorted other amenities, Minaki Lodge is ideal for muskie anglers who want to combine a serious fishing trip with a plush, Palm Springs-style vacation. For couples who enjoy muskie fishing together, Minaki Lodge is an ideal spot.

Best muskie lodges on the Winnipeg River

Minaki Lodge
Box 26
Minaki, ON
P0X 1J0
Ph: 807-224-4000

Gunn Lake Lodge
Box 20
Minaki, ON
P0X 1J0
Ph: 807-224-2321

Sunset Lodge
Box 25
Minaki, ON
P0X 1J0
Ph: 807-224-1092

Beaver House Lodge
Box 7
Minaki, ON
P0X 1J0
Ph: 807-224-1089

Big North Lodge
Box 24
Minaki, ON
P0X 1J0
Ph: 807-224-4318

Barber's Lodge
Box 37
Minaki, ON
P0X 1J0
Ph: 807-224-6411

Bayview Lodge
Box 21
Minaki, ON
P0X 1J0
Ph: 807-224-4301

Birch Island Resort
Box 5
Minaki, ON
P0X 1J0
Ph: 807-224-3471

Rainbow Trout

RAINBOW TROUT

Salmo gairdneri is one of Canada's most popular gamefish. Occupying a great diversity of freshwater habitats from coast to coast, the rainbow gets high points in all those criteria that make for a top-notch gamefish. It is difficult to catch, large enough to put up a good fight, it jumps readily, and it's delicious on the table.

The rainbow trout is a fish that wears many costumes. At the turn of the century, fish biologists collected so many rainbows of distinct coloration and physique that they assumed many different rainbow trout species existed. Biologists now recognize that rainbow trout is actually one species, with many strains or races. Rainbows are so adaptable they tend to change coloration and feeding habits in accordance with their habitat. Trout that inhabit the lakes of eastern Canada, for example, may feed primarily on alewives and other baitfish. Rainbows that live in the shallow, chilly rivers of the Rocky Mountains may feed almost exclusively on invertebrates (bugs). To further complicate the picture, rainbow trout that live across the continental divide may run out to the Pacific, swim thousands of miles, and grow to a whopping size. Anglers therefore use diverse strategies for catching rainbow trout, and these strategies are determined by the sort of habitat involved.

WHEN IS TROUT, TROUT?

Trout go by many names around the continent. Technically, lake trout and brook trout are members of the char family. But that particular distinction is not as confusing as some of the names these fish are known by. All of the trouts manifest different characteristics of size and appearance, depending on where they are found. Because of these differences of appearance, various local names have evolved.

The Chars

Lake Trout *(Salvelinus namaycush);* also known as Togue, Mackinaw Trout, Great Lakes Trout, Forktail

Dolly Varden *(Salvelinus malma);* Salmon Trout, Western Char, Bull Trout, Sea Trout

Brook Trout *(Salvelinus fontinalis);* Squaretail, Speckled Trout, Native Trout, Red-spotted Trout

The Trouts

Brown Trout *(Salmo trutta);* Loch Leven

Cutthroat Trout *(Salmo clarkii);* Salmon Trout, Harvest Trout, Mountain Trout, Blueback Trout

Rainbow Trout *(Salmo gairdnerii);* Kamloops Trout, Shasta Trout, Steelhead (when sea-run)

Fly fishing is the ultimate way to fish for rainbows. And the ultimate method of fly fishing is with a dry or floating fly. To fish for rainbows with a dry fly, an angler must "match the hatch," or present a fly that matches the current crop of insects upon which fish are feeding. Fly fishing for rainbows usually involves two kinds of habitat: rivers and lakes.

Mayflies, grasshoppers, midges, and a variety of other insects float on the surface when they accidentally land on the water, and sometimes these insects will be so numerous that the water is dimpled with their bodies. At times like this, trout will avidly rise to a dry fly.

Most often, however, trout stay submerged and feed on underwater aquatic life. It's far easier and more energy efficient for a trout to travel 6 inches to pick off a stonefly nymph, than it is to swim all the way to the surface for a floating midge. Therefore, wet flies are usually more effective when an angler is searching for trout and no hatch is underway.

Some basic tips for trout fishing are:

1. **Avoid periods just following a heavy rain.** Rivers will be murky from run-off.
2. **The first trout you keep may contain valuable information.** Perform an autopsy on the fish's stomach contents.
3. **When fishing a wet fly, make sure that the current doesn't push your line downstream of the fly.** It will drift unnaturally across the bottom.
4. **Streamer flies imitate minnows,** so they can be retrieved cross-current, as if swimming.
5. **Strike quickly!** Trout only mouth a wet fly for a second or two.

Stonefly

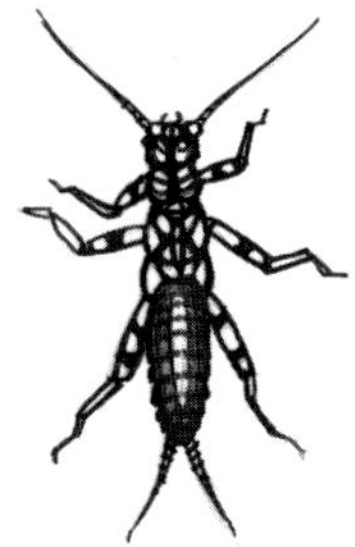

Nymph

Caddis fly

Worm (Caddis)

Caddis cases

Flies for Trout

There are three basic types of trout fly: *general flies*, which suggest a generic type of insect; *match the hatch flies*, which imitate specific insects; and attractor flies, which are flashy and colourful and arouse a fish's curiosity.

Anglers may prefer one type over another, but any well-stocked fly box contains examples of all three. Here are some basic flies to serve a variety of angling situations.

The Adams: With its neutral colour, barred wings, and mixed hackle, the Adams can pass for a variety of insects, including mayflies, caddis flies, and midges.

Grasshopper: During mid-summer, grasshoppers are an important source of food for trout. The best colour for hoppers seems to be yellow, and the simpler the design, the better.

Hare's Ear: Trout do most of their feeding underwater, so any basic fly selection should contain a number of underwater nymph patterns. The Hare's Ear has a long and mythic history in England, and is now one of the most versatile flies in North America.

Stonefly Nymph: These insects are such effective predators that they can become the dominant organism in a river. They spend up to 4 years underwater before maturing, so the underwater version of this fly is the trout's standard food.

Flying Black Ants: Late in the season, when aquatic insects are scarce, this terrestial insect is a favourite trout food. Flying ants may be blown into the water, where they flounder, half-submerged, making a tempting outline for a hungry fish.

RAINBOW COUNTRY

by Bob Jones

British Columbia's best-known outdoor writer is Bob Jones. With his snowy beard and fluid expertise with both fly rod and keyboard, Jones tends to make writing and trout fishing seem easy. They aren't. In this piece Jones gives us the low-down on his favourite place to catch rainbow trout in the west.

A chance meeting on Heffley Lake in British Columbia's Kamloops region once resulted in two boat anglers anchoring within speaking distance of each other. They were two of the area's best known anglers, professional fly tier and author Jack Shaw and biologist Brian Chan, manager of the Thompson-Nicola Region lake fisheries.

Their fishing techniques were similar. Each made a measured cast, then timed the line's descent with a wristwatch before starting a dead slow retrieve. Shaw's rod was first to lift against the weight of a trout, and the deep-bodied rainbow bounced erratically over the rippled water like a ball-bearing dropped on a marble floor. Chan appeared too intent on his own rod tip to notice, but as Shaw's net scooped up the 18-incher, he quietly asked, "What did it take?"

"Bloodworm," Shaw replied laconically.

Chan looked puzzled. "Bloodworm? That can't be right. Those are green chironimids hatching." He shrugged and continued fishing his tiny, sparsely-tied nymph. Minutes later it paid off with an aerobatic 15-incher he eventually released.

As the afternoon progressed, each angler hooked a dozen or so trout. Chan kept four, Shaw a limit of six. All were beautiful fish with the deep bodies and small heads typical of the rainbow strain local fishermen proudly call the "Kamloops trout."

The 36,000-square mile Thompson-Nicola region is a patchwork of open cattle range, heavily-forested mountains, and lakes – approximately 700 of them. According to Chan, about 90% of the lakes contain rainbows, and 10% have brook trout. Nearly 50 of the best known and most productive lakes lie within a 25-mile radius of the city of Kamloops.

"Kamloops is 1100 feet above sea level," Chan explains, "and the majority of the lakes

Angler in Heffly Lake with Kamloops trout.
Photo: Robert H. Jones

Trout flies (from top): Adams, Gold Ribbed Hare's Ear and Black Stonefly Nymph

are between 3300 and 4300 feet in altitude. We generally start off fishing the lower elevation lakes – about 1500 feet – and work up as the season progresses. By the end of June, when we're past the fishing peak, we're usually around 4700 feet."

That lakes near Kamloops stay consistently good despite periodic droughts and often heavy fishing pressure is credited to a combination of geography, water quality, and nutrients. Management also plays an important role. Twenty-seven of what Chan calls "quality lakes" have reduced limits, bait bans, and/or gear restrictions. The main requirements for restrictions are that a lake have the characteristics necessary to grow big trout in short periods, and be aesthetically pleasing to fishermen.

"Fish stocked during the spring in quality lakes are catchable by fall," Chan says. "That means trout going in at 2½ inches are upwards of 12 inches – and chunky – by fall. By the following spring those two-year-olds are 14 to 17 inches long and in good shape."

Low water has been a source of frustration for the fisheries branch, particularly between Merrit and Kamloops where popular lakes like Peterhope, Tunkwa, and Leighton were affected adversely in 1988. Chan said the three greatest dangers from reduced water levels are winterkill, loss of aquatic insect habitat along shorelines, and high water temperatures during the summer.

Although water levels are better than they have been for several years, the fisheries branch has several projects under way to alleviate future problems: diversions to direct more water into lakes, and new dams on some lakes to store water for release into others. A successful aeration program is also being expanded.

Despite some setbacks, the long range prognosis is positive. Stump Lake once suffered from high alkalinity and salt content that created losses with initial stockings. However, water levels have increased naturally over the past few years, diluting the salt content, and the problem appears solved. Stump is once again an excellent fishery, producing trout of up to 10 pounds and kokanee to 3 pounds.

Chan revealed that about 45 new lakes have been stocked with brook trout. "Strangely, they are underfished," he said. "Some have brookies of 7 and 8 pounds, which are trophy-sized anywhere. Fall spawners are notorious for being easy to catch, but in the spring it's different; they are rough, a real challenge, especially for fly fishermen. They can be harder to catch than rainbows."

Whether targeting rainbows, brook trout, or kokanee, anglers using spinning outfits should consider a lightweight rod loaded with a maximum of 8-pound test line. Popular lures in the area include Dick Nite spoons, small Flatfish (F3), Hot Shots, and Kwikfish in orange and black, plus various Rooster Tail, Mepps Blue Fox, and Panther Martin spinners in small sizes.

Trollers use everything from long gang troll and worm combinations to single spinners trailing a small lure or fly resembling a dragonfly nymph. A popular setup for kokanee is a small willow leaf gang troll ahead of a number 12 or 14 Spin 'N Glo.

Fly fishermen traditionally favour 5 to 7 weight outfits, but lighter rigs are becoming popular. The rod should be a minimum of 9 feet long for ease of casting while sitting in a small boat. Line selection should include floating, sink-tip, slow-sinking, and fast-sinking models. For fishing nymphs, leader lengths of 9 feet are sufficient, but some dry fly situations may call for up to 16 feet.

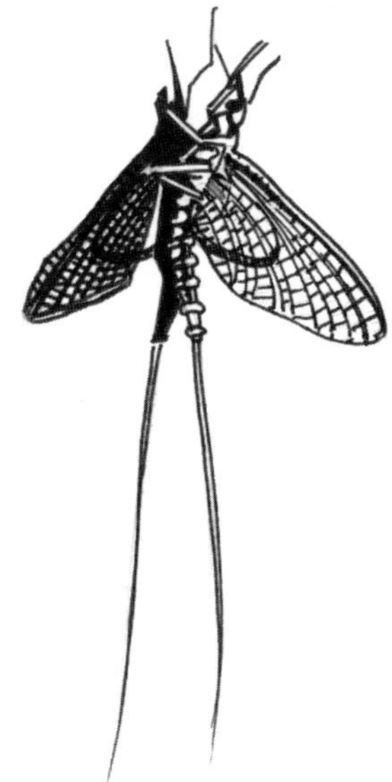

Mayfly

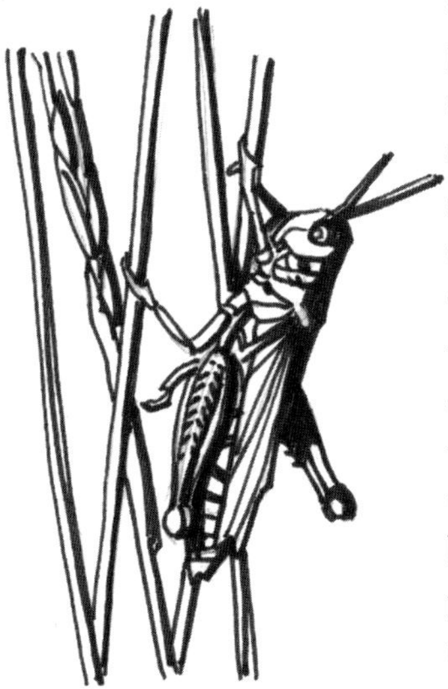

Grasshopper

Popular fly patterns, many developed by Jack Shaw, are available commercially in the area. These represent chironomids, damselflies, dragonflies, caddis and sedges in the pupal, larval, and emergent stages, freshwater shrimp, leeches, and backswimmer. Fishing starts right after ice-out, but Chan says it is short-lived. "Initially, we get three or four days of good fishing, then we wait for two weeks, depending on when the ice went off, for the water to warm up enough for the first chironomid hatch," Chan says. "As hatches occur at progressively higher elevations, we follow them up. That takes place during all of May, then around June 10 the first sedges start coming off – and damsels show up about the same time. They usually last into the first two weeks of July, by which time we're up to 4800 feet or higher.

Popular fly patterns represent chironomids, damselflies, dragonflies, caddis and sedges, freshwater shrimp, leeches and backswimmer.

"We have a summer doldrums period throughout August. The hatches are over and the water is starting to warm up. You can still catch fish, but it slows down until about mid-September. Then the water starts cooling again and the fishing gets good until freeze-up – the later the better.

"To narrow it down, the best time is between May 15 and the end of June, with the first 2 weeks of June being the peak period. Normally it's nice weather then, moderately warm rather than extremely hot, and it's also when you have the most exposure to all the different emergences.

"You have to tie in the time of day with the emergences. Several factors come into play, like evening sedge hatches, but generally the prime time is from 10 until 2 o'clock, when the sun is overhead. Personal experience and 15 years of keeping a diary have also taught me that the best action occurs during periods of a steady or rising barometer, but not on a falling barometer."

Kamloops area fishing situations include remote, hike-in, and fly-in lakes, and others accessible by 4WD dirt tracks, well-maintained gravel roads, and paved highways. Depending on location, accommodations vary from primitive public camping sites to commercial operations ranging from rustic to downright luxurious.

Some lakes have an abundance of trout under 10 inches, making them ideal for children and family outings, while others are strictly no-kill waters with trophy-sized trout reaching double-digit weights.

However, it is the lakes between these two extremes that are the region's main attractions, for despite natural disasters and increasing fishing pressure, they yield dependable catches of what many consider the strongest and most aerobatic of the rainbow strains – the high-flying Kamloops Trout.

How to Get There: Kamloops is 265 miles northeast of Vancouver, accessible by east or west via Highway 1 (TransCanada) or from the south via I-97 connecting to Highway 5. Air BC and Time Air have scheduled daily flights from Vancouver.

Where to Stay: Accommodations in and around Kamloops include four fly-in resorts, seven accessible by road, eleven campgrounds, and 34 hotels and motels.

Best Season: Mid-May until end of June, usually peaking during the first 2 weeks of June. Mid-September to freeze-up is also good.

Who to Contact: Tourist Information, Kamloops Travel Infocentre, 10-10th Avenue, Kamloops, B.C. V2C 6J7.
Phone: 604-374-3377

Best Knots for Fly Fishing for Trout

Fly fishing calls for a number of different types of knots. Some, like the improved clinch and the surgeon's knot, are covered elsewhere in this book. The **nail knot** is unique to fly fishing, and must be learned. Some knots are relatively simple and easy to learn. The nail knot is the other kind.

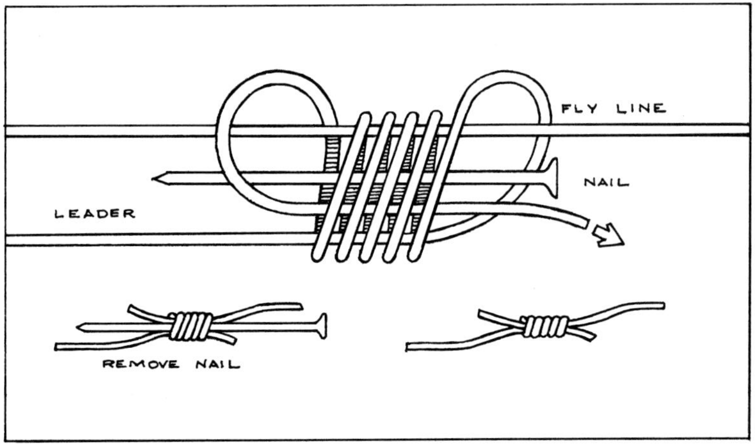

Nail Knot

The nail knot is a relative newcomer to the world of international high fashion in angling knots. The development of tough, plastic-coated fly lines has opened a window for the nail knot, which actually bites harder the more you pull on it. Nail knots are good for joining lines of different diameter, such as fly lines and backing, or fly line and leader monofilament. This is a difficult knot to describe verbally, and the best learning process is practice. Unlike other types of junctions, the nail knot is low-profile and doesn't make a bulky lump in the reel. It shoots smoothly and doesn't catch on the rod guides. To aid with tying the knot, anglers can use either a common nail, a piece of coat hanger, or a smooth section of twig. At the risk of stating the obvious, the nail is removed after the knot is completed.

DRIFTING THE BOW

North America has a number of famous trout streams. The Madison, the Beaverkill, the Ausable, the Two-Hearted, and many others have been celebrated in fishing lore and literature. Many the heated debate, too, has been waged over which of these famous streams offers the best trout fishing on the continent. Nowadays, the answer is probably none of them.

The best river fishing for brown and rainbow trout is no longer found in the United States at all, but in Alberta, Canada, on a river called the Bow.

The Bow spills out of the Rocky Mountains and runs down through the foothills into the city of Calgary. Once a dusty little cow town, Calgary has grown up into a wealthy, spanking-new city all aglow with western energy and oil money. Ducking out of the city, the Bow clips through rolling, wind-weathered hills of sage and willow. For about 60 miles east of Calgary, it provides ideal habitat for big, strong, fast, wild trout. Lots of them. On average, the Bow supports 1000 trout per mile. Browns outnumber rainbows three to one, and a chunky 20-inch fish is average. On a good day, a fly fisherman can bring two or three dozen to net. One storied woman hit the Bow on a blessed evening in June when the weather was fine, the insects were hatching, and her back cast was in the groove, and she proceeded to catch and release 206 trout before darkness fell.

One of the management policies that keeps the Bow trout population so healthy is an emphasis on catch-and-release fishing. The Alberta government stops just short of banning fish kills altogether (you're allowed to take home two in the summer), but many of the professional guides who work the Bow would like to see the river designated as catch-and-release only. The current president of the Bow River fishing guide's association is a bearish, easy-going outdoorsman named Mike Guinn. "There's a feeling among many anglers that eating a fish for supper is an important part of the sport. And I agree," says Guinn. "But the fact is, we have too many people wanting to eat a fish. Which do we want more? A meal or a good population of trout?"

Sally Kendall and Mike Guinn
Photo: Jake MacDonald

Guinn is a top guide, and a sort of modern-day mountain man. His mother married a famous pioneer named Soapy Smith, and they operated the Rafter 6 Ranch in the Kananaskis Valley. Little Mike became expert at an early age with both rifle and fly rod, and as soon as he was big enough he began guiding clients on 21-day sheep hunts in the mountains surrounding their ranch. Most of us have actually seen Guinn's family ranch, without realizing it.

Picturesque as it is, with split rail fences, log buildings, grazing horses, and awesome mountains, the spread has been used as a set in many Hollywood movies. Marilyn Monroe filmed *River of No Return* there, and the Disney corporation used it for movie projects such as *Wilderness Family*.

Like many avid young hunters, Mike Guinn loved animals and liked to live right among them. When he walked around the ranch he often had a fox trotting alongside or an owl sitting on his shoulder. The Disney people took notice, and invited him to come down to Hollywood and work for them as an animal trainer. He did. He worked with black bears, wolves, and grizzlies, and taught them to perform for all those famous Disney movies. But he found it hard fitting into the notoriously bureaucratic Disney regime. After seven years, he went back to Alberta and applied for three jobs: at the zoo, the Fish and Wildlife branch, and the Calgary Police. The cops returned his phone call first. "I got a call in the afternoon and was walking a beat that same night. They didn't have training in those days. They gave me a gun and a set of handcuffs and said, 'Away you go.' "

As a policeman, he won promotions quickly, and because of his expertise with guns and animals, eventually found himself managing the canine unit and the SWAT team. Throughout the years of his regular job, Guinn fished in Mexico, in Florida, in the far north, but mainly he fly fished in the Bow. Twenty-five years later, he retired from the police service and turned to his first love, fishing. "I had no intentions of working," he says. "But fly fishermen from the States would come up here. I'd take them out, and they'd insist on paying me. Eventually I figured, why fight it? So I became a fishing guide."

Guinn usually launches his home-made Mackenzie River boat (a double-ended row boat with high bow and stern) on the Bow a half-hour's drive east of Calgary. The river is tinted green with rock flour from the mountains, and Canada geese, mergansers, whistlers, and other waterfowl speed back and forth only a few wing-beats over the river. Once surrendered to the current, the boat quickly glides downstream, and Guinn plies his oars to give anglers time to work the pools and riffles that hold trout.

The Bow has an abundance of underwater invertebrate life, and that's one of the reasons the trout grow so large. On the down side, there's less opportunity for the dry-fly fisherman, because such a large percentage of a Bow River trout's diet is composed of nymphs, worms, and other submerged life. "This is a strong river," says Guinn. "And a trout has to budget its energy. If the fish can get a meal by hanging in the current and only moving a few inches, it's going to do that, rather than rise to the surface all the time for insects."

Guinn feels, however, that nymph fishing doesn't deserve second place in the pantheon of fly fishing. "It's much harder to catch a fish with a nymph," he says. "With a dry fly, you can see fish take. With a nymph, you have to develop a real sensitivity. That nymph is tumbling along underwater, at the end of a long leader, and the fish only takes it for a few seconds, then spits it out. I think that dry fly fishing is really a lot easier to master."

As we drift, the river is brown with heavy runoff from spring rains, but still we hit fish. Each is an energetic rainbow that jumps five or six times before being gently netted, photographed, and released. "With the river this muddy," Guinn says, "you have to put that bloodworm within an inch or two of a trout's nose. Most of the guides stayed home today. But you can always catch a few if you work at it."

After a few hours of drift fishing we pull ashore on a grassy meadow and Guinn prepares lunch: fresh bread, cheeses, meat, sliced onions, fruit, and a delicious lemon cake that he baked himself the night before. "I do all my own baking," he says. "It's a long day. Often, in the summer we'll fish until ten or eleven at night, and it's after midnight before we get to bed.

Then it's right back to work at six in the morning."

After lunch, it's time for lessons. Wading in the river we try to master the difficult art of casting a fly line into the wind, upstream, and getting it to drift downstream naturally enough to be accepted by a wary rainbow. Guinn, as big as one of his pet bears, slops around in the river in his waders trying his utmost not to lose patience with my utter incompetence. "Give it a mend, give it a mend, that's right. A big mend," he coaches tirelessly, peering over my shoulder. "Now strike it. STRIKE IT. Too bad . . . you missed a nice fish."

On all sides, the riverbank rises up in steep canyon walls, covered with grass and scrub willow. In the sand cutbank you can see the protruding white bones of buffalo that died here, hundreds of years ago. Geese wing overhead, honking sonorously, fleeing from a big dark thunderhead that looms over the canyon lip, grumbles and shoots a volley of rain pellets our way, and then sweeps off on other business. Blue skies follow. A blustery wind. Chilly. But the sandwich tasted great and what do you know, the casting is starting to find a groove. A Rocky Mountain whitefish takes my nymph and puts up a five-minute tussle, and then a lovely three-pound rainbow catapults out of the water with a red artificial in its jaw.

Releasing the trout, wading back into the water, I can feel the cold push of the river. Thigh-high is deep enough, thanks, for this cowboy. Like a trout, an angler's job is to find a good niche in the current and lock in. After all, none of us can accompany the river. A few days ago, it was climbing down off a mountain glacier. By tomorrow, it will have a good start on its journey back to the sea.

Mike Guinn
The Water Boatman
612 Queensland Dr. S.E.
Calgary, Alberta T2J 4G7
Phone: 403-271-0799

Lake Trout

Lake Trout

Lake trout are among the most beautiful of freshwater fish, and they are appropriately fussy about where they live.

Picture an eagle, tipping along a morning thermal. Down below is a pine-feathered granite cliff, and a tiny white boat puttering along through dizzily clear water. I had my introduction to lake trout about 20 years ago, working as a fishing guide, and the trees, blue water, and pine-tufted cliffs were the appointments of my office.

In those days every fishing guide carried a wooden crate and something called a "fish billy" in the bottom of his boat. We trolled with artificial lures, and the one that seemed to work best was Len Thompson's gaudy spoon, the Five of Diamonds. We dragged the spoons about 80 feet behind the boat. It was cold water, and the fish were up in the shallows. The spoons would flip and flash under the surface, and every once in a while there'd be a boil and one of the rods would look as if someone was hitting it with a two-by-four. My guest would chuckle, delicately place his cigar out of harm's way, then crank in another lake trout. I'd lift the fish out of the lake, whack it on the head, and throw it in the wooden box. For a few minutes afterwards, trolling again, studying the beautiful dying fish, I'd feel that one day this was something for which we, all of us, would be called to account.

I was right. The thousands of lake trout that my fellow guides and I bopped so offhandedly on the noggin were probably, in many cases, several years older than we were. Such reflexive overharvest was commonplace in those days, and was called "good fishing." As a result, many lake trout populations across the country have been wiped out.

Unlike most North American game fish, which spawn in the spring, lake trout spawn in the fall. Lake trout fishing seasons are closed in autumn to give fish a chance to move into shallow water and lay their eggs.

But the good news is that angling ethics have come a long way in the last 20 years, and it's now possible to keep one or two fish without damaging a lake's population. Given the delicious, delicate quality of a fresh-baked trout (stuffed with mushrooms and onions, rolled in foil, baked on a bed of coals while squirrels chatter and criticize, etc.), it's lucky that not even the most distraught of our biologists is suggesting we can't occasionally take a trout for dinner. Populations of lake trout aren't as high as they used to be. But reduced limits (two per day in many areas), angler education programs, and more conservation-minded, better-informed fishing lodge managers are relieving the problem. And as long as we have lake trout, that sizzling feast at shore lunch will undeniably continue to be one of the rewards of trout fishing.

Conversion Formula for Lake Trout

(use inches and pounds)

$$\frac{\text{length} \times \text{girth} \times \text{girth}}{800} = \text{weight}$$

Salvelinus namaycush favours the deep, cold waters of the Canadian north. In the summer, when surface temperatures rise, lake trout retreat to the deeper parts of the lake. This is not a matter of comfort but necessity, as lake trout cannot live in water warmer than 54°F. In winter, lake trout are distributed throughout all sections of a lake, including the shallow areas.

As spring progresses they retreat again into deep water. As the water cools in early October, trout migrate into shallow areas and prepare for mating. Males and females normally congregate along shoals and shorelines where deep crevices in jumbled rock and riprap provide their eggs some measure of shelter from predators. The legal fishing season, quite rightly, closes on September 30 to ensure that the trout get some peace and quiet on their honeymoons. But late September is an excellent time to crimp down the barbs on the old Five of Diamonds and intercept them on their way to the shallows.

Fishing is often based on the old strategy of match the hatch. Whether you're out for bluegills or mako sharks, it's a good opener to offer something that looks pretty much like the last thing your subject had for dinner. Trout lakes are cold, clear, and relatively devoid of life. Lake trout, therefore, are opportunistic feeders, which means they prefer to eat whitefish, perch, ciscoes, and smelt, but will settle for zooplankton, insects, and almost anything else that comes their way. Lake trout anglers generally fall into two camps: those who use bait and those who prefer artificials.

Minnows, worms, leeches, and grasshoppers make good bait for lake trout. In the autumn, when the waters are cold and the insects have tapered off, it's nice to go out on an Indian summer afternoon, sit on the pine needles, and watch your bobber. A strip of belly meat from a sucker is a treat that a cruising laker can't pass up. Last fall I took my laptop computer, wrote a story, napped in the sun, and took home a 5-pound laker. Anglers should know, however that catch-and-release fishing is difficult with bait. Trout often swallow the hook and you shouldn't be using bait unless you want a fish for dinner.

Artificial lures are just as effective and give you the option of releasing the fish. Rapala lures, Flatfish, Canadian Wrigglers, and most spoons will reliably catch trout. Trolling is a common method of presenting these lures, but in the warmer months lake trout are suspended in deep water, and the angler who misjudges the running depth of a lure is liable to waste a lot of time fishing where there simply aren't any fish. As the water cools in late summer and fall this becomes less of a problem, and anglers can troll experimentally in shallower water. In the far north, trout are never really in deep water, so depth is not a major problem.

Vertical jigging is a good method of

GO BARBLESS

Manitoba is one of the most progressive fish management jurisdictions in the world, and currently only barbless hooks are allowed in that province. Many other jurisdictions will be implementing barbless laws in the near future. And why not? Barbless hooks hold fish as well as conventional hooks if the angler keeps tension on the line and they are easier to remove. Fish caught on barbless hooks survive more often, and anglers waste less time performing dental surgery on fish they don't want to keep.

The largest lake trout in the world was 50 inches long and 44 inches in girth. It was caught in a commercial fisherman's net in Lake Athabasca in 1961. Its weight? 102 pounds.

prospecting for trout. Using a feathered jig or bucktail spinner, cast the lure and let it sink to the bottom, then simply crank it up towards the boat. Lake trout will sometimes hit the lure as it passes through the depth layer in which they are suspended. In northern lakes like Nueltin or Great Slave, anglers can stand up in the boat and cast for lakers just as they would for northern pike or bass. In the vodka-clear waters of northern lakes, there's no prettier sight than retrieving a yellow spoon, watching it flip along a few feet under the water, and seeing a couple of yard-long lake trout come finning behind it.

I still remember a fish that I caught that way one afternoon. It wasn't a special or extraordinary fish, just a nice, trim 12-pound laker with black shoulders and orange fins. The thing was, the day was just perfect. Sun beaming down, raven gliding overhead. Right in the middle of an idyllic northern summer. I held the fish up, admired it, and then whacked it on the head. We ate it later, cooked over a driftwood fire, and the meal was truly fine. I had no apologies to the fish. As Clark Gable's cowboy pointed out in Arthur Miller's great story, *The Misfits*, "Nothin' lives unless somethin' dies."

But if I'd let that fish go he'd still be swimming in those crystal clear waters, 20 years later, and wouldn't that be a great memory too?

Tips for lake trout fishing:

1. **Lake trout move into shallow water during spring and fall**, and are then easier to catch. A few weeks after ice-out is probably the best time of the year.
2. **In summer, search for lake trout with a graph**, if possible, to determine their depth.
3. **With no graph, anglers can jig vertically.** In this method, the lure travels through all depths on its retrieve.
4. **Don't hesitate to release trout caught in deep water.** Walleyes suffer from the bends if retrieved from deep water, but lake trout do not.
5. **Metal spoons are an ideal lure.** Trout like to eat small ciscoes and whitefish.

Five of Diamonds

The Five of Diamonds

On a bright sunny afternoon in the Canadian northwoods, walk up to any group of anglers or fishing guides and ask them about their favourite lure for lake trout or northern pike. Many of them will say, "the Five of Diamonds."

The Five of Diamonds spoon is yellow with five diamond-shaped red spots. It's such a successful lure that most manufacturers of metal spoons put out a model in that colour pattern. In fact, the Five of Diamonds pattern rivals the red-and-white daredevil pattern as the most popular coloured spoon of all time. Prices vary according to the manufacturer, and in bargain-basement stores, you can purchase these spoons for less than a dollar.

Imitation may be the sincerest form of flattery, but most serious anglers agree that imitations of the Five of Diamonds don't catch as many fish as the original. The original Five of Diamonds spoon was invented many years ago by a man names Len Thompson. History is driven more by coincidence than by design, and the invention of the world's most famous trout spoon occurred because of a twist of fate.

During the First World War, a regiment of Canadian soldiers was dug into a line of muddy trenches near the Belgian town of Ypres. One day, from the direction of the German line, a greenish-white blanket of fog came rolling in over the barbed wire and entered the Canadian trenches. It was chlorine gas. Lines of startled infantrymen fell to the ground, kicking and choking. By the time the fog lifted, 5,000 young men were dead. Len Thompson was one of those Canadian soldiers, just barely into his 20s, but he was one of the lucky survivors.

Shipped back to Canada, young Thompson was ordered by his doctor to go out to western Canada, where the air is fresh and clean, and spend as much time as possible outdoors. Thompson took this to mean that he was under official orders to go fishing for the entire summer. So like Nick Adams, the hero of Hemingway's famous story "Big Two-Hearted River," Len Thompson limped off into the woods and valleys of the northern wilderness, looking for a cure for the nightmares of war.

Money was scarce, and Thompson made his own fishing lures out of wood, carving them by hand. Gradually he became more interested in metal spoons, convinced that the flash of a spoon attracted fish more effectively than a wiggling plug. He turned an old shed into his machine shop where he built a few hundred metal spoons from car springs he'd scrounged from the local dump. The spoons seemed to catch fish successfully, and he kept improving the design, basing the spoon's flash and wiggle on the critical reviews he got from local fish. The next year, he travelled around to local fishing camps, selling the lures on consignment.

The lure caught on. And today, the Five of Diamonds spoon is still being manufactured. Len Thompson's grandson runs the plant, which employs six full-time staff and produces about 700,000 lures annually. Ironically, the Five of Diamonds spoon is a name invented by fishermen. In the company literature the lure goes by the somewhat less dramatic label of the "YR model – Yellow and Red." The lures are punched out on a press, and then polished in soap and water while small steel balls deburr them. After drying, they are hand-painted with lacquer and then baked to a finish. The split

Lake trout grow very slowly, often less than half a pound per year. A 30-pound trout may, therefore, be quite a few years older than the angler who caught it.

The lake trout's scientific name *(namaycush)* is a native Indian word meaning "dweller of the deep."

rings and hooks are mounted and hand-tested, and then the lures are packaged and sent to market.

The Thompson-Pallister Bait Company is now located in Lacombe, Alberta, where the naturally soft well-water is an excellent medium for polished lures. The company still manufactures the Five of Diamonds (okay, the "YR – Yellow and Red") according to Grandpa's original specifications, using high quality steel it brings in from Noranda, Quebec. Until his death in 1979, Len Thompson himself attached the hooks and split rings to the Five of Diamonds spoons, and also managed the company's public relations department. On file in the company archives are numerous letters from faithful users, such as 65-year-old Mr. Dorwin Lamkin, from Kansas. After 19 years, he caught so many big fish with the same Five of Diamonds lure, including a 35-pound salmon and a 38-pound lake trout, that the spoon was worn out. Rather than throwing it away and buying another one, which Mr. Lamkin felt would be the same as sending "a hardworking old horse to the fox farm," he requested that his Lucky Five of Diamonds be rebuilt. The company repainted his lure, fixed it with new hooks, and sent it back to Mr. Lamkin with the stipulation that they would be glad to rebuild it again, free, if he promised to put it to work for another 19 years.

Thompson-Pallister Bait Co.
P.O. Box 940
5124 - 47A Street
Lacombe, Alberta T0C 1S0
Phone: 403-782-3528
FAX: 403-782-3533.

When the Len Thompson spoon first came out, the advertisements used to say that "Fish like it so much you have to hide behind a tree when you're tying it on your line." Most experts agree that if you're going fishing up north for big lake trout, you'd better make sure that you've got a couple of beat-up old Five of Diamond spoons in your tackle box.

Windy River Outpost Camp

Dan Sisler, from Ithaca, New York, was fishing out of Windy River Outpost Camp on July 22, 1992, when he hooked and released a trophy lake trout at Fox Narrows. The fish measured 48 inches in length and 27 inches in girth, weighing 43 pounds and 11 ounces. The fish was caught on 12-pound monofilament line, in 17 feet of water, and was netted after a struggle of 15 to 20 minutes.

Dan and his fishing partner for the week, John Eriksen, also of Ithaca, were fishing with a pink Dardevle lure purchased the day before at the outpost camp. It was a very successful week for the two fishermen in that they also caught and released five lake trout over 30 pounds, and eight lake trout over 20 pounds.

Dan is a veteran of many fishing trips to the Northwest Territories, although this represented his first trip to Nueltin Lake. Dan's success despite his being visually impaired is a tribute to his abilities as an experienced fisherman.

Photo courtesy Richard Koelling

Nueltin Lake Lodge

HERE BEE MONSTERS . . .

On the old navigational maps used by 14th-century sailors, vast regions of the globe were dismissed with a simple warning: "Here Bee Monsters." We may laugh today at such superstitions, but in fact there are still plenty of places in the world where monsters do exist, and where Nature has a chilly welcome in store for bright-eyed travellers.

The farther north you go in Manitoba, the more you begin to feel like an intruder. The landscape becomes increasingly vast and forbidding. Sub-arctic rivers braid and unravel beneath the airplane's wing. Thousands of no-name, uninhabited lakes glint like hammered copper under a smoky, cold sun. The sky thickens with shaggy, rolling cloud. At the border of the Northwest Territories, all signs of contemporary human civilization have long since been left behind, and a huge, disorganized flood of post-glacial water sprawls across the patchy-green planet. This is Nueltin Lake. And here indeed be monsters.

Inhabiting Nueltin Lake are some of the biggest lake trout and northern pike in the world. Years ago, the managers of Nueltin Lake Lodge instituted one of the first really serious catch-and-release policies in North America and, as a result, the giant fish of Nueltin are as numerous as they've ever been. Except for a few small ones that the guides keep for shore lunch, all big fish, like the 56-pound lake trout bagged

“With all due respect to the long-heralded waters of Great Bear Lake and Great Slave Lake in the Northwest Territories, the finest place today for catching a lake trout over 20 pounds, and even over 30 pounds, is Nueltin Lake.”

—Ken Schultz, Associate Editor, *Field & Stream*

recently, are released unharmed. If an angler wants to mount a trophy, measurements of the big fish are taken and the taxidermist makes a moulded trophy, more durable, more realistic-looking, and about the same price as an old skin trophy. When anglers visit Nueltin, they can be assured that the giant lakers that swam in Nueltin last year haven't flown south in some angler's ice-chest last week.

There's no commercial fishing on Nueltin and 40 anglers are spread out over a wilderness lake 120 miles long. Guests fly direct from Winnipeg (about a 3-hour flight) via large turbo-prop Hawker-Siddely aircraft, which land at the lodge's 5000-foot strip. Guests can choose between three camps: one main five-star resort (Treeline Lodge) and two outcamps (Windy River and Nueltin Narrows). Guests at Treeline Lodge use full American Plan, with guides and meals provided, while outcamp guests run their own boats and cook their own meals, at a lower price of course. All boats have new outboard motors each year and are equipped with swivel seats, life jackets, nets, paddles, and electronic fish locators. Prices have remained level for the last three years, making Nueltin one of the best values on the fishing market.

On a typical day of fishing at Treeline Lodge, guests awaken to a fresh pot of coffee delivered to their cabin. Breakfast, with fruit, home-made pastries, bacon, eggs, toast, and everything else, follows in the large dining room, with its big windows overlooking the lake. Your guide might be someone like Norman Denechezhe, a Chipewyan (Dene) guide from Lac Brochet who has spent half his life working as a Nueltin Lake fishing guide. You might go fishing up the Windy River, a winding, rapid-laced watercourse with grayling and lake trout lurking below each riffle and boulder. As Norman pilots the boat expertly through white horses and gravel bars, you'll see hills covered with wildflowers and lush grasses, stunted spruce trees and wheeling bald eagles, and perhaps a herd of velvet-antlered caribou swimming across the river.

On shore, deep ruts are paths where caribou herds have migrated for centuries. Rings of stones show where Norman's ancestors pitched their tents beside the migrating herds. At the mouth of Windy River, a tumbledown cabin is the site where Farley Mowat wrote *Never Cry Wolf*. Less famous, but no less interesting a character was Ragnar Jonsson, a truly legendary trapper and outdoorsman who spent most of his life alone, wandering the barrens around Nueltin Lake, and whose old campsites can still be found around the lakeshore. When asked if he enjoyed the big city, Jonsson would confess that he liked to go to town "every ten years or so." With only a canvas tent to keep him warm in –40°F weather, Jonsson slept with his sled dogs, lived off the land, survived into his 80s, and was a colourful hero to northern Manitoba's bush pilots, nurses, and flying RCMP.

At noon, after a morning of great fishing, Norman or one of the other guides will pull the boat onto shore and prepare a delicious lunch of fresh fish, cooked over a crackling bonfire. Want to stretch your legs? The low bushes on the hillside are laden with blueberries,

Windy River outpost camp

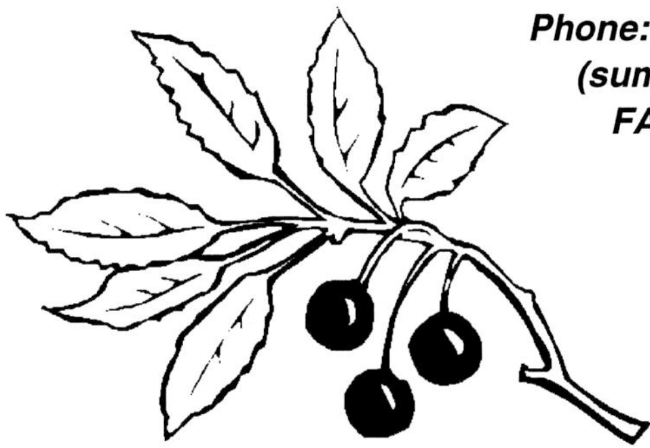

Nueltin Fly-In Lodges Ltd.
P.O. Box 1561
Morden, Manitoba R0G 1J0
Phone: (winter) 204-822-4143
(summer) 204-284-3247
FAX: 204-822-6484.

cranberries, and black currants. After packing down a great lunch of hot beans, trout fillets, onions, potatoes, and dessert, you want to lie down on the soft moss and grab a wee nap in the hot afternoon sun. But somehow you'll summon the energy to climb into the boat and go searching for more big fish.

At the end of the day, it's time to head back to the lodge. Dinner, drinks, the fireplace, and good conversation await. Not a bad way to spend a week, if you can stand it.

Call Me Ishmael

The Native residents of Lac Brochet watched Garry Gurke trying to wrestle a caravan of heavy equipment through the mid-winter bush, and dubbed him the "crazy white man." Like Captain Ahab, another crazy white man, Garry Gurke believes that the biggest fish of all time lurks in the bottom of Nueltin Lake, and he's nailing a reward to the mast for the first angler who brings the fish in. Nueltin Lodge offers a standing reward of $5000 for the angler who catches and *releases* an all-tackle world-record lake trout. The angler who wins the gold doubloon might catch the Big One in June, around the river mouths, while the main lake is still covered in ice. The lure? A big spoon with a single barbless hook. He'll be smart to keep the tension on the line, especially when the fish is near the boat. One shake of the head, one mistake, and that monster will disappear, leaving the poor angler with just another far-fetched Big Fish Story for the dinner table.

PLUMMER'S LODGES

You can't talk about lake trout fishing without talking about the Northwest Territories, and Plummer's Lodges.

The two biggest, deepest, and most forbidding lakes in the Canadian arctic are Great Bear and Great Slave. Great Slave, the smaller of the two, is nevertheless 300 miles long and 150 miles wide, a monstrous expanse of ocean blue with places where there's half a mile of deep, very cold water under your boat. The best place to fish for lake trout on Great Slave Lake is Taltheili Narrows, a 400-yard-wide hourglass linking McLeod Bay with the main body of the lake. In early summer, large lake trout migrate through Taltheili Narrows and early in the morning you can see them rolling like dolphins on the misty surface. Plummer's Great Slave Lodge sits right on Taltheili Narrows, and guests at the lodge have the best fishing on Great Slave Lake right outside their door.

Great Bear Lake is one of the biggest freshwater bodies in the world, and is widely recognized as being the most productive lake trout waters in the world. Dease Arm, 47 miles north of the Arctic Circle, is the best and most productive section of Great Bear Lake, and, just as at Great Slave, this prime section of the lake is the location of Plummer's Lodge. Two year ago, Plummer's Great Bear broke the world record for lake trout (again) with a 74-pound fish (released), and since most of the big fish caught at Plummer's are released, it's likely that another record-breaking trout will come out of Plummer's soon.

In the Canadian north, the Plummer family is a sort of mythic equivalent of the Ewings of "Dallas." Warren Plummer started the first camp in 1938, after searching the Arctic for a truly exceptional place to catch lake trout. He

settled on Taltheili Narrows, and built a four-man camp there that has grown into Great Slave Lodge. Warren's son Chummy Plummer now runs both camps, and an out-camp on the Tree River besides. Chummy runs the camps all summer, flies out regularly to test-fish remote lakes, hits the sports show circuit in the winter, and manages to squeeze in an occasional hunting trip to Argentina or Botswana or someplace similar when he gets a chance. Like his dad, Chummy doesn't mince words. He runs a very efficient camp with good equipment, serious Dene guides, top-notch airstrips, and excellent food. When the Plummers first

---

Tree River Char Camp

Arctic char live in the ocean and perodically run up into fresh water to spawn. Although there are good char rivers around the shores of the northern world, the best is located in Canada, the Tree River. There's only one lodge on the Tree River, and it's owned by Plummer's.

The Tree is a wild river with many rapids and white-water pools. Guests fly in from Great Bear Lake Lodge on a DC-3 and stay in four-person tent cabins, with wooden floors, beds, heaters, and down sleeping bags. Since the river is good all along its length, individual guests do not require guides. Pathways alongside the rapids allow guests to fish when they want, where they want. And because the sun burns 24 hours a day, you can fish for char until your arm falls off. The trophy? A scarlet fish that makes a beautiful photograph and a gourmet meal when you get home. Tree River char average 12 to 14 pounds, much larger than at any other place in the world, and anglers are allowed to take home two apiece. The Tree River camp is available only to guests of Plummer's Great Bear Lake Lodge.

built their camp at Great Bear, they discovered that most of the good fishing was a long boat ride away at Dease Arm. Most camp operators would have coped with this somehow, by offering fly-out trips or making do with the merely exceptional fishing right near the lodge. The Plummers, true to form, put all their lodge buildings on skids and hauled them across the ice to the best spot on the lake.

Apart from the fishing, both lodges offer spectacular scenery and wildlife. Huge cliffs and soaring eagles rise from crystalline blue waters that are so pure you can see the boulder-strewn bottom at 40 feet. You mix your drink with water scooped right out of the lake, and at shore lunch, while the guide makes a delicious meal of fresh trout over a crackling fire, guests may look up into the woods and see a bear, sitting behind a tree, waiting for the boat to leave so he can come down and see if there are any leftovers. Guests come and go in modern Boeing 737 jet aircraft, and after a week of catching beautiful trout, taking in the scenery and the power of those awesome lakes, there's no stranger experience than sitting in an airport in Winnipeg or Minneapolis, listening to the Muzak, with a slight smell of lake trout on your fingers to prove that the whole thing wasn't a dream.

Plummer's Lodges
950 Bradford Street
Winnipeg, Manitoba
R3H 0N5
Phone: 204-774-5775
U.S. Toll Free 1-800-665-0240
FAX 204-783-2320

My FAVOURITE Place in the WHOLE WORLD

by Cam Hurst
former head guide
Plummer's Lodges

I've fished and hunted just about everywhere on this goddamn continent. And I've never seen a place as pretty as this little group of islands on Great Bear Lake called the Narakays. You got a beach there made of round stones, a little U-shaped bay, and the sun beating down on this pure clear water that you can see every grain of sand in 50 feet. It's like being in the South Pacific. There's good trout fishing here. I'm not talking great fishing, but good fishing. When you've caught as many fish as I have, you start to put some value on other things. So to make a long story short, I just love going to those Narakay Islands.

Wayne Gretzky used to come up to Plummer's and I took him out fishing. He's a nice kid. When you sit in a boat all day with somebody, talking about politics, sports, what makes life worth living, you get to know that person pretty well. Once day at the end of his trip I asked him where he wanted to go fishing. There were lots of places to catch a real trophy. But Wayne thought for a while, then he smiled at me and said, "Let's go to those Narakay Islands."

Channel Catfish

CHANNEL CATFISH

This large and hard-fighting member of the catfish family *(Ictalurus punctatus)* is easily distinguishable from other members of the catfish family by its deeply forked tail. It also has a distinctive blue-grey skin, covered with dark spots.

Like all catfish, the channel cat uses its barbels to search for food – normally minnows, worms, crayfish, and insects. Channel catfish spawn in dark cavities along muddy river banks, and the female defends the young when they first hatch. Channel catfish have white, tender meat that is prized in the United States, particularly in the south, where large catfish farms produce millions of pounds annually without satisfying public demand.

The all-tackle world record for channel catfish is 58 pounds, but a 20-pound fish is generally considered to be a trophy. Across North America, they are found in warm, rock-bottom rivers in relatively deep cover. In clear water, they are mainly active at night. In murky water, they may feed actively during the day.

Although catfish are large and fast, they often take a bait quite gently. Anglers usually mistake the first tentative nudge of a giant catfish and assume that it's a little one. But anglers should always set the hook firmly anyway. Catfish have a leather-tough mouth and big fish are often lost beside the boat.

Channel catfish anglers don't need a boat or fancy equipment to get started. A pole, a can of worms, and a comfortable spot alongside a riverbank are about as complicated as catfishing needs to be. Anglers wait for the tell-tale tug of a nibbling cat, then they free-spool their reels and let the fish run with the bait. When your line stops feeding out, the catfish is getting ready to swallow, so that's the time to set the hook. The best time to fish for channel cats is morning and evening; and the most promising place in North America to catch a truly monstrous specimen is the Red River, in the province of Manitoba.

Some tips for catching channel catfish:

1. **Channel cats have no difficulty swimming in fast water, but they like to hang slightly out of the flow** behind obstructions, while the current brings food to them.
2. **Anglers can search for these pockets either with a graph or by watching for rolling fish.** When a fish is caught, the angler should memorize the spot.
3. **If no catfish hits your bait within 15 minutes, cast to another spot.** Fish are usually stationary, and delivering a bait to their doorstep works better than waiting.
4. **In the Red River, the best month is June.** The best weather is overcast, with a north wind. The harsher the weather, the better the fishing.

Equipment:

Seven-foot bait-casting rod and good quality open-face reel with star drag, loaded with new 17-pound monofilament; at the terminal end, a sliding 1-ounce sinker above a barrel swivel, and an 18-inch leader tied to a wide-gap, No. 4 barbless Eagle Claw single hook.

The Owl and the Pussycat
Channel catfish have few predators except for human anglers and horned owls. An owl will cruise the surface of the river in darkness, scoop up a small channel cat, and enjoy a fine dinner in some riverside tree.

For the LOVE of a CATFISH

Manitoba's Red River is the best place in the world to catch a big channel catfish, and the best guy to introduce you to one of those big fish is a 40-year-old Métis fishing guide named Stu McKay.

On any windy, cloud-wracked day in early spring Stu McKay can be found in his fishing boat just a few hundred yards downstream of the Lockport dam, an hour north of Winnipeg. Brown water thunders through the spillway gates, a hundred white pelican wheel overhead, fish splash and roll in the tumbling current, and McKay, wearing a drover's Stetson pulled low above a weathered face, wears a pearly smile as one of his clients grunts and wrestles with another big catfish.

Channel cats can be found throughout the Red River system, but two Manitoba towns, Emerson and Selkirk, claim the title of "Catfish Capital of Canada." There's a varying opinion on where the best fishing actually is. A ballet dancer I know released one of the biggest catfish in

Manitoba last year, and he says that the best place to catch huge cats is actually in downtown Winnipeg. Stu McKay, on the other hand, likes to work the stretch of fast water just below the Lockport dam, where it's not unusual for his guests to catch, in one day, a dozen catfish averaging 18 pounds apiece. The Red is a big river, running maybe 90 miles from the American border up to the lake where it empties, and a little dissension over the hot spots helps to spread the anglers around.

Stu McKay

Photo: Wayne Glowacki, Winnipeg Free Press

Channel cats are extremely strong. Before going after them, check your tackle. Where is the first place this set-up is going to break? Are you using last year's line? Flimsy swivels? Is your drag dirty or corroded? When a 20-pound catfish decides to leave the neighbourhood, he doesn't care who you know. Fix those glitches now instead of afterwards.

Stu McKay got started in the guiding business on a part-time basis, 20 years ago. At that time, Manitoba's catfish population was unknown to most anglers, and McKay can take some of the credit for popularizing his home locale as one of the greatest fishin' holes in North America. Recently a number of increasingly enthusiastic journalists from as far away as Hawaii and England have discovered the Red River, producing a little whirlwind of publicity, and now it's a rare day between spring and fall that McKay isn't booked with a group of serious lifetime catfish anglers, wealthy businessmen, or pro baseball players from Kansas or New York City.

He loves his work and seems utterly devoted to the ugly, whiskered monsters that he spends his days pursuing

As the market has grown, McKay and his wife Diana have tried to keep up with the demand. They have recently taken over Lilly An's, a traditional boat-launch and hot dog stand a quarter-mile downstream from the Lockport dam. There they do land-office business selling fishing licences, bait, tackle, parking spots, and hot chocolate to anglers who come to meet the Red River channel cat face to face. McKay doesn't charge much for a day of guiding, but he seems to enjoy the work so much that he probably feels guilty about being paid at all. Guiding, like all jobs, eventually becomes a matter of slaving over a cold river, sucking exhaust smoke, shivering, staring at that punctuation mark where one's fishing line disappears into the mirror. But McKay watches the birds, watches the water, fusses with his presentations, and maintains a constant enthusiastic patter on the subjects of river biology, weather, cloud movement, and who makes the best motor. He loves his work, and seems utterly devoted to the ugly, whiskered monsters he spends his days pursuing.

"I try to encourage everyone to practise catch-and-release fishing," he says. "When we catch a big fish, I keep it in the net and quickly free the hook. Unless someone wants a picture, we'll have that big cat swimming away again in about a minute. In the old days, there were no limits. And people would sometimes come up here, fill up the back of a pickup truck with chipped ice, and go back to the States with maybe a thousand pounds of catfish. Nowadays, conservation is foremost on everyone's mind. And because of that, the fishing is getting better every year. You really have to try it to believe it."

Stu McKay Outfitters
Lot 109 River Road North
Lockport, Manitoba R0C 1W0
Phone: 204-757-9876

Best Bait for Catfish

There are almost as many types of catfish baits as there are catfish anglers. Some enthusiasts swear by doughballs. Others use chicken livers, night crawlers, shrimps, catfood, or well-aged stinkbaits created by sealing meat into jars and letting it sit in the sun.

Stu McKay probably catches more record-sized catfish than any guide in North America, and he swears by a simple piece of goldeye. McKay catches small goldeye (12 inch) right below the Lockport dam with a worm and bobber combination. But any oily fish will probably work as well for catfish bait. McKay slices the goldeye into 1-inch-wide steaks, and puts the bait on a #4 hook behind a slip sinker.

Smallmouth Bass

SMALLMOUTH BASS

Micropterus dolomieui is one of the most important gamefish in North America, mainly because of its cocky temperament and acrobatic behaviour when hooked.

Smallmouth bass don't grow to a great size – a 5-pound fish is a very large specimen – but a bass of that size will put on an unforgettable display. Many anglers rate the smallmouth, pound for pound, as the scrappiest fish that swims.

At one time, smallmouth bass were confined to a relatively limited area around the Great Lakes and the Ohio valley. But they have proved hardy and adaptable, as well as pugnacious, and over the years they've hitch-hiked across the country by whatever means available. Many travelled by railroad. The legions of bass now inhabiting the Potomac basin, for example, all descended from a few fish that rode across the Alleghenies in a bucket on a Baltimore and Ohio freight train. In many lakes, smallmouth have been introduced by a process no more complicated than someone, usually an angler, carting in a barrel full of fish and pouring them into the water. In many cases, the bass take over the lake. Today smallmouth bass are established in an area bounded by Quebec, Alabama, Oklahoma, and in the west, the Pacific states.

Bass spawn in late spring, when the water temperature reaches about 65° F. In the north, this is usually around the first week of June.

During the spawn, the male digs out a shallow depression in the gravel with his tail and then attempts to drive ripe females towards the nest. Once the female lays her eggs she is dismissed and the male goes looking for another mate. Up to three females may lay their eggs in the nest, and then it is aggressively guarded by the little male. During the incubation period of about a week the male will attack anything that approaches the nest, including a fishing lure. Bass are therefore easy to catch during the spawn, but it's a hard-hearted angler who doesn't release most of the fish caught during this period. In most species, the male is the expendable one. But anglers who want to keep a fish for dinner should remember that with smallmouth bass, it's ladies first.

Once the water warms up in mid-summer, bass become harder to catch. Food, in the form of insects, minnows, and crustaceans, becomes more abundant and the angler's lure has many competitors. Also, bass move into deep water and the angler who hopes to catch them with surface lures should be up at daybreak, when the lake is glassy, the water cool, and the fish are more likely to be in shallow water. Come September, bass return to their shallow water haunts along the shoreline and fishing improves. Many bass anglers believe that autumn offers the best bass fishing of the year.

Conversion Formula for Smallmouth Bass

(use pounds and inches)

$$\frac{\text{length} \times \text{length} \times \text{length}}{1600} = \text{weight}$$

Here are a few tips to answer that old question, "What went wrong?" while fly-casting for smallmouth bass:

Problem: Fly hits the water on the back cast.
Solution: Make the back cast more briskly. Keep your wrist locked and the rod tip high.

Problem: The line develops knots after casting.
Solution: Wind knots are caused by punching the rod during the forward cast, or from flicking your wrist. Try to apply power smoothly and, again, keep your wrist locked.

Problem: Line piles up and collapses at end of cast.
Solution: If you use a wide casting arc, say from 9 o'clock to 3 o'clock, you'll build up a wide loop that doesn't transmit power well. Instead, keep the casting arc tight and brisk by locking your wrist and keeping the rod tip high. Take a look behind you on the back cast and watch the line in the air.

Problem: The fly snaps off the end of the leader.
Solution: Wait until the line straightens out on the back cast before applying forward power. Look over your shoulder and watch the line unfurl to get the timing.

Bass on the Fly Rod

One day when I was deep within the seething termite mound of midtown Manhattan, I visited Orvis, alleged to be the most prestigious fishing-tackle store in the world.

The clerk, a gent in a tweed grouse-hunting jacket and silken cravat, showed me a split-bamboo fly rod priced at the nice round figure of $6,000. Whipping it mischievously in the air, I asked him if a rod like this was as durable as any good, run-of-the-mill hundred-dollar graphite.

"Sir," he scolded quietly, "You don't acquire a rod like this for its *durability*. It's a piece of art."

In the minds of many anglers, that's precisely the trouble with fly fishing. For years it's been associated with images of private clubs, snappy fashions, and gear that has as much to do with artistic pretensions as with catching fish. Most anglers look on a fishing rod as a tool, plain and simple. And they want to own a rod that's well-suited for the species they pursue. In years of fishing I'd never seen anyone catch a walleye or a pike with a fly rod, so I'd never felt much desire to buy one.

As fate would have it, however, an in-law from Chicago mailed me an old-time English fly-fishing outfit as a Christmas present (worth considerably less than $6,000). So I called my friend Bruce Ranta, who works as a biologist with the Ontario Ministry of Natural Resources (MNR) in Kenora, and asked him if there was any practical use for it, beyond gazing on it as a work of art.

To my surprise, Bruce, who also happens to be an enthusiastic fly fisherman, told me that most of Ontario's gamefish species can be caught effectively with a fly rod. "Insects are natural prey for most of our fish, and the best way to present an artificial insect lure is with a fly rod," he explained. "People have always used fly rods for trout, but now anglers are realizing that they're a great way to fish for pike and bass." The MNR encourages anglers to pursue bass with a fly rod, because it's trying to take some of the pressure off walleye. "You should try it sometime," Bruce said. "I know some lakes where the smallmouth bass go crazy for a fly."

I thanked Bruce for the invitation, and told him he could pick me up on Saturday morning. In the meantime, I realized that I'd better do some homework.

Fly fishing may be a somewhat esoteric pursuit nowadays, but it seems that once upon a time it was really the only technique in use.

Fly fishing had become a well-established sport by the 1600s, and a London businessman named Izaak Walton wrote a book that to this day is regarded as the finest volume ever produced on the subject. In *The Compleat Angler*, Walton describes the dozen-odd basic flies that a fly fisherman needs, calling them his "jury of flies, likely to betray and condemn all the Trouts in the river."

Walton pursued trout by standing in rivers and streams, while Bruce Ranta and I would be fishing for smallmouth bass from a boat. But many of the same principles, techniques, and flies can be used for both species.

In Walton's day, rods were made of split cane, but nowadays good, medium-weight fly rods are made of graphite and can be purchased for under $100. A seven-and-a-half to eight-foot #6 or #7 rod is all you need. Look for the stiffness rating on the shaft, near the grip. Unlike spinning reels and baitcasting reels, which have complex gears and drag systems, fly reels are very simple and are used mainly as spools for storing line. Some models have no drag at

Fly fishing can be as expensive – and difficult – as you want to make it. However, you should be able to get a good-quality graphite rod for less than $100, and a basic fly reel can cost as little as $30.

Ian James, a registered instructor who teaches both fly tying and fly fishing, explains that the basic fly casting motion should come from the forearm, not the shoulder. Keeping your wrist locked and your forearm straight will take you a long way towards good casting form. Don't use your shoulder muscles as you would with a baseball throw. Keep your rod tip high, and move the rod back and forth. "It's a slow, relaxing rhythm," James explains. "It should almost lull you to sleep." The idea is to keep the line in the air, and not have it plop into the water on every forward and back cast. If you let your wrist break, the rod will point down, and your line will go in the drink. However, if your first attempts go awry, don't try to correct things in mid-cast. "If it doesn't work, stop and regroup." says James.

all. Fly reels are therefore relatively inexpensive and won't add much to your set-up costs. Prices start at about $30. Tackle retailers will tell you that it's important to purchase a good spool of floating fly line that is matched by weight to your rod. Simply match the number on your rod to line with a corresponding number. For example, a #7 rod takes #7 fly line.

Once your reel is loaded with Dacron Backer line and about 30 yards of floating fly line – Double Taper Line, which is fattest in the middle and tapers off towards both ends is a good choice for beginners because it's accurate and forgiving – all that's missing from your bass rig is a leader. And, of course, some flies.

The leader usually consists of a piece of 8-pound monofilament, 8 to 10 inches in length. Traditionalists will insist that no leader is complete without a "tippet" – a short length of lighter monofilament used to improve the way ultra-light flies cast. But with the kinds of flies I'd be using to catch smallmouth, I learned, a tippet really isn't necessary. Fly casters experiment with different combinations of line and leader, since some cast more effortlessly than others. But it's not necessary for a beginner to go into that much detail. Fly fishing is one of those pursuits that can be as difficult as you want to make it, and a simple set-up will work well for cottage-country gamefish.

When it comes to lures, bass are opportunistic feeders, preying on grasshoppers, worms, crayfish, and just about anything else they can stuff in their mouths. For bass fishing, tiny floating dry flies will work, but you're better off to go with floating bass bugs that imitate frogs, grasshoppers, and the like, or sinking wet flies that imitate nymphs, crayfish, and larvae. Flies and bass bugs are inexpensive as lures go ($2 to $4 apiece), and a selection of four or five is all you need.

My basic set-up was complete when Bruce picked me up on Saturday morning, and while we drove to the lake he explained a few basic principles of casting with a fly rod. "With a baitcasting or spinning rig you throw the lure," he said, "and the lure's weight peels off the line. When you're casting with a fly rod, the lure weighs practically nothing. So you have to rely on the weight of the *line* to cast the lure." Bruce went on to say that casting fly line is a very awkward experience at first, since most anglers are accustomed to casting lures rather than a long, looping curve of line.

In fact, the first thing you should do is unlearn all your regular spincasting habits.

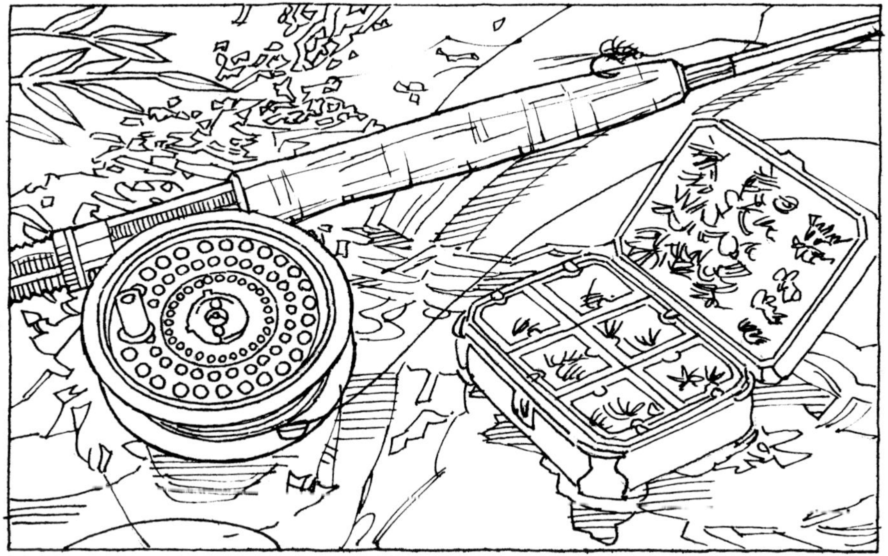

Some instructors go so far as to teach righties to cast with their left hands, forcing them to learn a new motor skill.

"The bass are ready to do their part," Bruce promised, "if you can manage to deliver a fly to them."

Some anglers tend to endow sportfish with almost super-natural intelligence, but expert fly fisherman Ian James is more down to earth. "You"ve got to remember that you're trying to catch something that has a brain the size of a pea," he says. "A selection of four or five flies is all you need, and you won't have to bust open the kids' piggy bank to buy them."

Our bass-fishing location was, oddly, Pickerel Lake, northwest of Kenora, a medium-sized, spruce-rimmed beauty, flat as pavement under a steady drizzle. We motored across the lake and pulled into a quiet, glassy-calm bay with a large, fishy-looking boulder down below, and I soon learned the frustrations of learning to fly cast. Bruce tied a small hair frog onto his leader and pointed towards a sunken log. "I'll bet there's a bass right there." He stripped eight or ten coils of line from the reel and let them lie in the bottom of the boat. Holding the line in his left hand, he switched the rod back and forth overhead, until a long loop of line swished out and the bass bug settled on the water. He left it sitting there. "Okay, you try it," he said.

I did exactly the same thing, except that my fly unaccountably embedded itself in the rim of my hat. "Try it again," Bruce said. "Let the rod do the work. Don't force it. You should keep the rod tip high and let the line straighten out on the back cast. Look over your shoulder and watch it unfurl."

The next cast went a little farther. It described a bizarre loop-the-loop and snagged in the landing net. Bruce looked nervous. "It's raining," I said. "Why did you just put on your sunglasses?"

"I should have got you started with a piece of yarn," he replied. As I untangled my fly, he explained that beginners are well-advised to spend a few hours practising in the yard, with a tiny snippet of yarn on the end of the line, before graduating to a hook. The yarn is safer than a real fly and keeps the end of the line from fraying. On my third cast, the bass fly hit the water several feet from the log. As if on cue, a smallmouth immediately smacked the fly and disappeared, peeling line off the reel and bending the long buggy whip of a rod. My reel didn't have a slip drag, so under Bruce's frantic instruction I palmed the reel with my hand and gave the fish some friction to pull against. When the bass slowed I reeled in the line, using the crank handle just as you would with any other reel. Soon the bass tired and Bruce lifted it by the jaw. "Two and a half pounds," he said in admiration. "Nice fish."

"I think I've got the hang of the casting too," I said, whacking a fly into the sleeve of Bruce's jacket.

Learning to drop a fly gently and accurately into a precise pocket of water 80 feet from the boat requires more than the space of a magazine article. A plethora of books and articles explain the basics of stance, follow-through, and so on, but there's no substitute for practice. In any case, the fish themselves don't seem to care much about technique, once that feathery tidbit hits the water. During the next drizzly few hours, Bruce and I bagged and released so many smallmouth bass that I felt as though we were conducting a poll. Most of them weighed in around 2 pounds. But we also caught half a dozen 3-pounders. All danced, jumped, and tail-walked in that famous smallmouth style.

"I think I've go the hang of casting too," I said, whacking a fly into the sleeve of Bruce's jacket.

We were dressed in good rain gear, but a heavy downpour eventually finds your bones no matter what you're wearing. Unscrewing my thermos, I poured a cup of hot chicken-noodle soup and observed my bass fly, floating on the still, rain-dimpled water. As if sucked down by a tiny vacuum, the grasshopper suddenly disappeared. I picked up the rod, bumped the hook, and the biggest bass of the day roared out of the water. After a few minutes he was tuckered enough that we could photograph and weigh him (almost 4 pounds) and put him back in the water. I smiled at Bruce. "So how am I doing professor?"

"No more instructions," he said. "You're starting to annoy me."

Topwater Bass Lures

Smallmouth bass are accustomed to plucking food from the surface of the water. In fact, so much bass food – bugs, frogs, wounded minnows – adheres to the surface of the water that topwater lures are one of the most effective gimmicks for taking bass.

Bass feed most actively in the morning and evening, and during those periods the water is usually calm and glassy. But bass don't require calm water conditions to hit topwater lures. As long as the water is quiet enough to show the action of a topwater lure, bass will react.

Topwater lures fall into a few general categories. **Stickbaits** like the Rapala can be used as wounded minnow imitators. Fished on the surface, twitched, and retrieved in slow stages, a small Rapala is extremely tempting to smallmouths.

Poppers feature thick bodies and concave faces. When twitched, they make a gurgling pop in the water. The Hula Popper is a venerable version of this lure. Most likely bass see these lures as a frog, so anglers should try to imitate the dart-and-pause motion of a swimming frog as they retrieve.

Propeller baits, as the name suggests, feature cigar-shaped bodies and tiny whirring propellers. The Tiny Torpedo is a favourite propeller bait. The famous Zara Spook is closing in on its hundredth birthday, but it still catches bass.

Anglers should avoid casting directly to logs, lily pads, and other cover that may conceal bass. Topwater lures make a good splash when they hit the water and they scare fish if they strike the water too close. If the water is calm and glassy, lures should be fished gently. A twitch, a pause, and a slow retrieve work best.

In choppy water, a rougher retrieve is better for attracting bass. The most important thing to remember when using topwater lures is to pause when a fish hits, and then strike. The most frequent cause of losing fish on topwater lures is striking prematurely. Admittedly it's very hard to resist a knee-jerk reaction when a bass engulfs your lure, but it's necessary to wait until the fish dives underwater before setting the hook. Count one thousand, then strike.

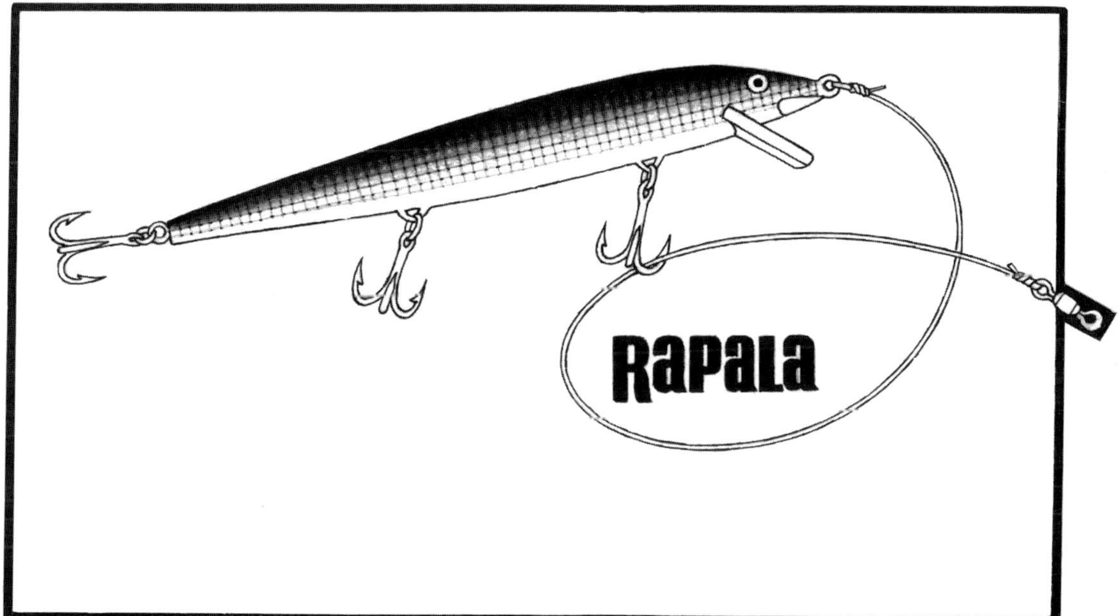

Rapala lure

Chinook Salmon

CHINOOK SALMON

Students of fish biology call this fish *Oncorhynchus tshawytscha*. Or at least they're supposed to, if they hope to get full marks on their orals. The coastal peoples are a little more poetic. In the Haida language, the chinook salmon is the "little swimmer." Meanwhile, according to whimsy and who's doing the talking, the same fish might be called the "spring" salmon, the "king" salmon, and the "tyee." By any name, *Oncorhynchus* is the largest and most impressive salmon in the world.

In the Pacific Northwest, chinook salmon are sometimes confused with coho salmon, which are the second most common fish caught in that part of the world. Chinook, however, are larger. A fish of 30 pounds is considered a tyee salmon, or trophy. And an average-sized chinook weighs about 18 pounds. Coho, on the other hand, attain an average size of 6 to 12 pounds. A large coho can be differentiated from a chinook by its teeth. Coho have needle-like teeth that are white at the base. Chinook salmon have loose, conical teeth that are black at the base.

All this may seem like hair-splitting. But anglers employ substantially different methods for pursuing each species. Coho are fast-swimming, active fish that hunt near the surface.

Anglers therefore watch for surface activity from seabirds, and move their lures at a quick troll (4 to 8 miles per hour). Chinook salmon generally travel much deeper in the water (50 to 100 feet) and prefer a slow-moving lure, (1 to 2 miles per hour). The most successful lure is probably the cut-plug herring, which is a small herring rigged to wobble lazily when trolled. The purist method of rowing up a tyee, however, is to use an artificial lure, usually a metal spoon, slow-trolled behind a double-ended rowing skiff. A 30-pound tyee, caught by this method, is regarded by anglers as the trophy of a lifetime.

In recent years, the great rivers of the Pacific Northwest have come under increasing pressure, and chinook salmon populations are in serious trouble. Japanese drift netting, heavy commercial harvest, power dams, and siltation of spawning streams have combined to push many west coast salmon populations to the brink. Most recently, a series of controversial Supreme Court decisions have granted aboriginal fishermen the right to harvest and sell spawning salmon without regard to seasons or limits. All these user groups are pitted against each other, and while they squabble, salmon continue to decline.

In the United States, chinook salmon populations have already collapsed. In 1969, the winter run of chinook in California's Sacramento River was estimated at 188,000. Last year, biologists counted all the returning fish they could find. The total spawning population? One hundred and ninety-one. Before the Columbia River was dammed, back when it was one of North America's purest and mightiest rivers, the salmon run numbered about 20 million fish. Now about one percent of those fish survive. In British Columbia's Fraser River, the same drastic decline will certainly occur if salmon consumers don't bring their harvest down to a sustainable level.

In the meantime, British Columbia still provides the best chinook salmon fishing in the world. The south coast area, particularly the Georgia Strait, has mild weather, top-notch luxury accommodation, and easy access to international airports. The oldest and most distinguished fishing resort on the B.C. coastline is Painter's Lodge, next door to the Tyee Club, one of the most famous fishing organizations in the world.

The north coast, particularly the region around the Queen Charlotte Islands, is a wilder, colder, and wetter place to fish. But the salmon are enormous and abundant. To ameliorate the hardship of sitting out in a small boat all day while trolling for salmon in the drizzling rain, many north coast lodges have built "tender boats." These are large (in the 100-foot range), well-appointed cruisers which play mother hen to waterlogged anglers. With this system, anglers needn't make long trips every morning in small boats – and a bowl of hot soup is never far away.

British Columbia provides the best chinook salmon fishing in the world. The south coast has mild weather, top-notch luxury accommodation, and easy access to international airports. The north coast is a wilder, colder, wetter place to fish. But the salmon are enormous and abundant.

It's a rare opportunity to step off an airplane into a boat and to be salmon fishing half an hour later. And meanwhile be gazing at misty fjords, spouting whales, and a backdrop of snowcapped coastal mountains. But visiting paradise comes with responsibilities. And because of the antagonistic climate that characterizes Pacific salmon harvest, until recently fishing lodges have been slow to implement wise conservation policies. Everywhere across Canada, the best lodge operators now insist upon catch-and-release of trophy fish. Some lodges allow anglers to keep one trophy. Others insist that anglers put all big fish back in the water. Taxidermists only require a fish's measurements, plus a photograph, to make a quality mount, in any case. But on this front, British Columbia's salmon lodges are still oddly rooted in the past. Brochures show anglers lined up on the pier with a body count of huge salmon, and the importance of conserving such beautiful fish is never mentioned. "At one time the lodges took an insignificant number of salmon," explains one Department of Fisheries and Oceans biologist. "But there's more lodges now, and the numbers are getting up there. The lodge owners feel that if they don't kill the salmon, someone else will."

Another biologist puts it more bluntly. "We might as well be out on the last buffalo hunt. When the fog clears, someone will be standing there laughing, saying 'I got the last one.' "

For most people, a salmon is just something to eat. But anglers truly love the chinook salmon. They don't pursue the fish for profit, as so many others do, and a boatload of fish needn't die in order for the angler to have an enjoyable morning on the water. Tourist outfitters across Canada once feared that anglers wouldn't tolerate catch-and-release policies, but they've since learned that most of their customers are good sports. In this day and age, most responsible people accept that nature's resources are finite. If the mighty chinook salmon is going to survive into the 21st century, anglers should be the ones leading the battle to save them.

What can anglers do? A good place to start is to ask a few simple questions, when shaking hands with your lodge manager.

"Do you encourage your guests to release large chinook salmon?" If the answer is no, you might well ask another question: "Why not?"

Conversion Formula for Chinook Salmon

(in pounds and inches)

$$\frac{\text{length} \times \text{girth} \times \text{girth}}{800} = \text{weight}$$

This knot is a simple and effective way to join two lines of different diameters.

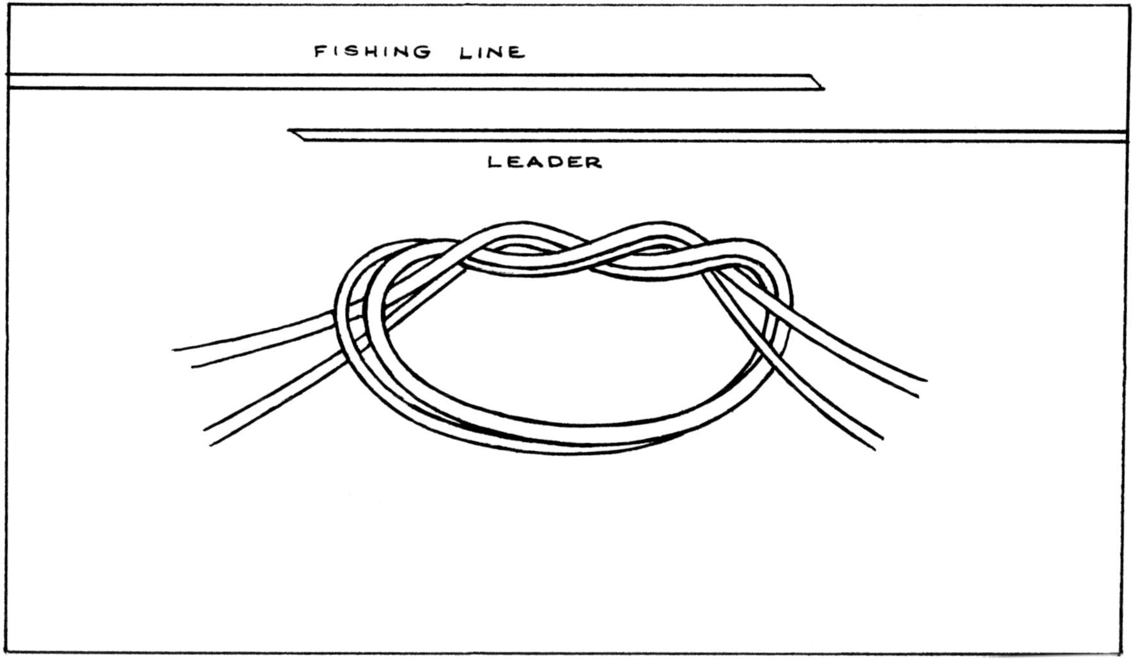

Double Surgeon's Knot

The Gibbs Spoon

The Gibbs Spoon

In British Columbia, where the snow-capped mountains run like saw teeth above the cold blue waters of the Pacific, five species of salmon draw anglers from all over the world. If you walk down to the docks in the morning and see a fishing guide hunched over in the rear seat of a trolling boat, polishing something that looks like a piece of sterling silver cutlery, it's probably a Gibbs spoon.

There are numerous good salmon lures on the market, but the Gibbs spoon or, more correctly, the Gibbs-Stewart spoon, is one of the most venerable and popular salmon lures ever developed. In 1908, a company called the Gibbs Tool and Stamping Works started up in Vancouver, B.C. The owner was Rufus Gibbs. A tireless innovator and hard-nosed businessman, Gibbs quickly became successful at producing prosaic items like pipe hangers and floor plates. But Gibbs, a bachelor, had passion to spare and he poured his real enthusiasm into sport fishing and lure design. Gibbs' company was only a 5-minute jog from salt water and he found it easy to field-test his designs on real salmon. As backup, Gibbs relied on advice from professional guides and fine-tuned his spoons to perform more effectively in the field.

Today, there are many cheaply made spoons manufactured in Asia, and while low-priced spoons may look just like the higher-priced models manufactured in North America, subtle difference in design can make a big difference in performance. Up on the famous salmon fishing grounds near Campbell River, there are historical references to guides making small improvements to the Gibbs spoon: "a young professional tyee guide named Herbert Pidcock files the front end of his spoons to give them a slightly sharper taper, which in turn gives them a slightly quicker wobble when trolled." Pidcock's advice to other guides was to buy a dozen standard spoons, file the front ends and "expect to get three from the bunch that will actually work." Herbert Pidcock was one of the finest fishing guides to ever troll the waters off Campbell River, so it's not surprising that Rufus Gibbs incorporated the young guide's advice into the design of the standard spoon.

In 1935, a 64-pound tyee set a new record at Campbell River's prestigious Tyee Club. The fish was caught by John Agnew of Seattle on a No. 7 Gibbs-Stewart spoon. In 1936, Rufus Gibbs himself won a gold and bronze medal from the King Salmon club of Comox, for catching eleven coho and four tyee salmon (ranging from 30 to 46 pounds) on his own spoons.

The Gibbs-Stewart spoon, and a range of other products, made Rufus Gibbs a millionaire. But beyond fishing, he had few hobbies. He was a fixture in Vancouver's old Patricia Hotel for 42 years and never owned a TV or drove a car. At the age of 77, Rufus Gibbs took his spoon out for one last run, and caught a 41-pound chinook salmon.

Long Live the KING

By David Carpenter

I've always wanted to write a novel starring a huge, mythic and evil-tempered Northern Pike. David Carpenter went right ahead and did it. He didn't even ask my permission! Here, Carpenter scores another first. He tells a great story about an experience we all dread: getting skunked.

Tyee is a Salish Indian word meaning "the mighty one." The chief. When a chinook salmon gets to be 30 pounds or better, it becomes a tyee. In British Columbia, an entire corporation has been built on this fish, and its most illustrious fishing camp is Painter's Lodge in Campbell River.

Painter's Lodge is the spiritual home of the Tyee Club, the most venerable fishing derby in Canada. For almost a century, around the end of August, anglers have been coming here, hoping to catch a tyee and join the club. The King of Siam, Glenn Ford, Zane Grey, Bud Abbott, Bob Hope. All have sought to distinguish themselves in an utterly primitive fashion: by killing a mighty salmon.

At Painter's, a sort of Taj Mahal of fishing camps, past glories are evident in every room. Photos of men and women with their tyees, buttons emblematic of valour in the cause of salmon fishing, trophy tyees on the wall, old spoons and plugs in glass cases. The photos have a ghostly quality. Writer Roderick Haig-Brown, known more for his love of fishing than for his considerable ability to bring them in. Thomas Caldwell Litler-Jones from the Channel Islands, gold button winner in 1929, when he caught a 54-pound salmon, and later, with a 45-pounder. Mrs. R.L. Cobb, Tyee Man of the Year in 1931, the first in an impressive line of women to win the honour.

Painter's Lodge takes its name from master boatbuilder Ned Painter, who could build one of his patented 14-foot clinkers in 50 minutes. The design is so stable that there was never a drowning in the estuary from a Painter boat. The one possible exception to this cannot be blamed on Painter's design. In 1937 or '38, two brothers from Saskatchewan apparently convinced their guide to take them out into the tumultuous waters of Seymour Narrows and were never heard from again.

The town of Campbell River, of course, lives by its fish. One of the keenest anglers is the manager of fishing operations at Painter's, Wayne Dreger. He speaks with the nervous energy of a dynamite blaster, and when he describes the technique of striking a tyee, his entire body seems to tense up like Boris Becker before a serve.

"You watch that rod tip," he lectures us, perhaps conscious that we are not precisely two brothers from Saskatchewan, but close enough. "You don't take your eyes off it. You may want to talk to your buddy, but that doesn't mean you can take your eyes off your tip. Remember, this is not fun. It is utter concentration. The very second your tip flutters, you strike as though your life depended on it."

My buddy for this trip is an old friend from Vancouver, Pete Nash. Already he has located our guide and rower, a young man named Randy. He tells us to be ready the next morning by 5:15 a.m. After a wake-up call at 4 a.m., Nash and I drift outside, in a west coast wooze of fatal memories. Randy is out on the wharf. We are going fishing. As they say out here, we are going to row a tyee.

The Tyee Club rules state that fishermen

must not use a motor while fishing. Our rowboat has a motor, but we can only use it to get out to the area, maybe half a mile long by a quarter-mile wide, that we're going to troll. It's a flood tide, so we're heading to the Tyee Pool in the south side of the river mouth. An ebb tide and we'd more likely row Frenchman's Pool on the north. The salmon congregate there, testing themselves against the strong and tricky currents as they prepare to head upriver to spawn. By gentleman's agreement, the two pools are reserved for Tyee Club rowers.

Nash mans the motor while Randy gets the tackle ready. We are using 7-foot rods with single-action reels, 20-pound test line, and large Gibbs-Stewart spoons. Randy is forever shining these spoons as if they were pieces from the royal family's tea service. Randy is obviously the right man for the job. In many ways he is an ordinary guy, but in matters of angling, he is a perfectionist.

We skim over the chuck, and the night begins to lift from the estuary. Shapes loom out of the dark: islands, rocks, hills. We have entered an outdoor gallery of Toni Onley sketches that drift out of the twilight in a dream of yammering gulls. Randy waves a hand at Nash to cut the engine.

My rod tip bobs up and down with the dodging rhythm of the spoon. I hold my thumb on the spool of my single-action reel. When the rod tip flutters, I will not feel the strike. But I will strike back nonetheless. I will yank that thing back so hard I will almost break the rod or my back. Nash is thinking the same thoughts, I am sure. Grim. We are a disciplined duo and we are not – absolutely not – having fun. Neither the gentle weather nor Randy's unfailing good humour will alter our Prussian demeanour.

"Nash, having fun?"

"Nope."

"Good."

"How about you, Carp? Having fun?"

"Nope."

"Good."

Our first shift ends around 8:30. Just as we are turning to go for breakfast, Randy looks up from polishing my spoon. "Dave," he says, "did you feel anything out there this morning? Even a nudge?"

"Not a thing. Why?"

"There's a tooth mark on your spoon."

I didn't kill a tyee salmon. We saw them though. Rolling out of the ocean like economy-sized orcas or slapping the surface with their tails. They were there, huge and beautiful, too huge to imagine lying comfortably in our small boat. Too beautiful to imagine dead, a mere trophy emblematic of some guy's manhood. Even my manhood, which I had almost forgotten about. Seeing the big salmon roll made me wonder. Like the keenest anglers in the Tyee Club, I am trying to kill this creature I admire so much – not by purchasing a tin of salmon at the supermarket or by any other act of consumer boredom – but by fooling it with my patience and my art. Killing a mighty fish is not a moral act; it's a primitive act. Don't be fooled by the cane rods and the tweed coats worn by the old anglers of the Tyee Club. Yes, they are gentlemen, but when they take or harvest or beard or finesse a salmon, the verb they use is "kill." Killing a mighty salmon takes us back, however briefly, to our most primitive origins when fishing well meant eating well. The man or woman beholds how fat and deep the body, how silver the sides, how perfectly streamlined the salmon for long runs and mighty leaps. It may have been the first angler at the dawn of time who looked at the fish and said "tyee."

Well, Nash and I were skunked. Randy offered us a frozen salmon but having, I suppose, our pride, we turned him down.

But my adventure has a postscript. Alone in my car on the last leg of my journey back to Saskatoon, I had a strong urge to throw out the old fly line. I did a little detour to a lake known for its bruiser rainbows. I had no boat, but I knew of a spot where you can flycast from shore without your backcast getting fouled.

I guess you know what happened. On the first cast from shore my fly landed about 35 feet in front of me. I waited while it bobbed on the surface, then pulled it under and began to jerk the fly towards shore. There was a monumental surge where my fly had been and I saw a dark back and the flash of a big dorsal. My reel was buzzing and my fly was being carried at violent speed towards the center of the lake. When I checked the first long run, the rainbow swam right for me and I had to strip in line as fast as I could. The fish wheeled and did a slow leap out into the blue terrific sky. It seemed to hang there in defiance of gravity and re-enter as softly as an otter sliding into a pool. I think it's fair to say that it too was "tyee," in another one of his magnificent guises. The Chief had come to call.

It took about 15 minutes to tire the fish and 5 more to head it into a shallow channel. Two feet long, as deep-bodied as its Pacific cousins, and built for power rushes and acrobatics. A 10-pound rainbow trout. These are about as common as large emeralds in your back garden. But I released the fish without hesitation. Who was I, after all, to presume to spill the blood of the Chief? Unhooked, the fish lay stunned and exhausted in the channel, righted itself, and with a shudder from its powerful tail, ploughed away from the shallow water leaving an impressive wake behind.

I had a very pleasant drive across the prairie all the way to Saskatoon. I had only one lingering doubt in my mind: When I walked into the kitchen with an empty cooler to tell my wife, Honor, that I had just released the biggest rainbow either of us had ever seen, would she believe me?

Painter's Lodge
Oak Bay Marine Grp.
1327 Beach Drive
Victoria, B.C.
V8S 2N4
Phone: (Toll free)
1-800-663-7090,
(Collect)
604-598-3366,
FAX 604-598-1361

The Stuff of DREAMS

By Gordon Pyzer

Gordon Pyzer and Bob Izumi are two of Canada's best-known anglers. Pyzer works for the Ontario Ministry of Natural Resources and spends much of his spare time looking for the best places in Canada to go fishing. Here, Pyzer tells the story of a memorable expedition for Chinook Salmon.

Let's daydream for a moment. Imagine a small dot on the map where tens of thousands of huge, wild salmon run as thick as marmalade. Imagine a giant funnel for the last great migrating masses of fish. Exquisite silver-sided salmon on their way home to British Columbia. Mature chinook and coho back-tracking to the sweetwater rivers of their birth.

Now fill in the scenery with deer, bear, seals, sea lions, peregrine falcons, soaring bald eagles, and pods of killer and grey whales. And there's no ignoring the ancient Haida totem poles or the towering Douglas firs or the red cedars seemingly glued (they must be) to the rocky walls that dive into the Pacific.

Finally, imagine a fishing lodge that's a veritable floating palace with hot tubs, lounges, and crackling fireplaces. And it floats in a peaceful cove where the water is so clear blue you can watch starfish crawl across the ocean floor from your third-floor balcony.

Now you've got it. But it's no dream. It's Langara Lodge.

Langara Island and its lodge sit like a crown on top of the Queen Charlotte Islands. They're way up there on our west coast, with only a stretch of water called Dixon Entrance between them and the Alaskan Panhandle. I spent five fantastic fishing days there last September with Bob and Wayne Izumi. We came away shaking our heads over the wonder of it all.

The lodge was built to take full advantage of the rich heritage of salmon fishing around Langara. The owners did their homework and picked the site very carefully. Says the co-owner, Rick Bourne: "We knew the fishing was going to be good but we never dreamed it would be this good. From our camp alone we catch more tyees (chinook over 30 pounds) than any resort area in British Columbia.

Bourne's words were still tumbling in my head as our three boats pulled away from the dock one afternoon. Our destination, fittingly enough, was a grey stone point called Coho Rock. I was sharing a boat with the guide, Jeff Bottay, and as we moved through an ebbing tide, he explained the finer points of "motor mooching." You point the bow of the boat into the onrushing current of an ebb tide and, periodically, you drop the motor in and out of gear. "That way, you won't troll too quickly. And your cut herring bait will spin in a slow, tight wiggle."

As we talked, I kept one corner of my eye on how Bob and Wayne were doing in the other two boats – I knew they were doing the same. Even among the best of friends, it's every man for himself when the fishing is this good. Wayne was the first to get lucky.

There was a good 100 yards between our boats, but I could still see Wayne's rod tip flicking back and forth, as though a light-biting walleye or bass was pecking at his bait.

Best Time to Go

The fishing season normally runs from the third week in May to the last in September. There's good fishing anytime, but late May and June are your best bets for a heavyweight spring. June also offers a lot of fishing time – the sun rises at 4:00 a.m. and sets at 11:00 p.m.

Coho show up in July and salmon anglers treasure the acrobatic silvers for their high-flying, heart-stopping leaps. The average weight of early coho is about eight pounds, but after feeding ravenously for a month, the majority of them are pushing ten pounds or better.

Bob and I were using traditional west coat gear: 11-foot, medium-action graphite mooching rods and matching single-action reels. But Wayne – ever the experimenter – had set out purposefully to land his first Langara salmon with his favourite bass-fishing equipment. Just to prove it could be done.

I watched him hit the free spool button on his baitcaster and feed out line to the fish tapping his bait. Then he dropped his rod tip sharply and retrieved a few yards . . . slowly . . . until he felt some resistance. Next thing I knew, he reefed back so hard that I swear he skipped the boat over an incoming wave.

Meanwhile, I had spotted Bob tensing up in his boat. His rod tip was doing the same wild tap dance. He quickly stripped out line from the giant reel and fed it to the fish. I watched closely and counted one, two, three fast rips. Then Bob stood up, planted his feet squarely on the floor of the boat, and attempted to pull the plug out of the bottom of the Pacific Ocean. Not a chance. The plug was alive and hightailing it across the Dixon Entrance for the only land in sight – the southern tip of Prince of Wales Island and Alaska.

Bob's fishing partner, Rick Bourne, began to reel in like mad so they could chase the big fish. But halfway back to the boat – pow! Another big salmon had mugged Bourne's twirling herring.

Jeff Bottay slipped our motor into neutral and whispered: "Get ready. There's a school of big fish moving in and any moment now. . . ." Before he could finish, I was onto one.

There are essentially two ways a schizophrenic Langara salmon strikes your bait. It can slam so hard that your rod feels like it's about to shatter and splinter in your hands. But more often, it pecks away at the rotating herring and feels just like a tiny panfish.

Jeff Bottay watched my rod tip quivering gingerly. "Three pulls fast," he yelled. I yanked out mono. Still the salmon pecked away at its dinner, like a kid poking at a plate of liver and spinach, knowing there is only custard to anticipate for dessert. "Easy now," said Bottay. "He's just playing with your bait."

My heart was pumping and I was hyperventilating. Instinct told me to plaster the big, teasing sonofagun, but experience said no. Two years before, I'd fished for Team Canada in a five-nation salmon tournament, and I knew that you have to keep your rook and wait for the king to make the next move.

Finally, Jeff Bottay gave me the go-ahead. "But don't rip too hard," he warned. "Reel in slowly and when you feel the fish, just sweep-set the hooks. They're razor-sharp."

I tightened up until I felt the throbbing salmon. It was like someone whacking a tennis ball on the end of a dangling string. But the next time the salmon hit my bait, I cupped the reel tightly, so that the line wouldn't unravel and tangle, and swept back. Straight away, my rod doubled into the ocean and my reel spun like a runaway mixmaster. I yanked my fingers away from the whirling handles – they don't call them "knuckle busters" for nothing.

Next thing, Bottay let fly with a blood-curdling holler that almost knocked me out of the boat. It was his salute to what he called a "screamer" fish. Wayne's fish, he said, was a tough barroom brawler, slugging it out deep below, but both Bob's salmon and mine were screamers. As I held onto the bucking rod for dear life, he explained that salmon from different rivers often fight very differently. And after my fish had kicked and punched me around unmercifully for ten minutes, I had a few things to say about its spawning ancestry that I can't repeat. It felt absolutely marvellous.

Best Time to Go

Silvers peak in both numbers and size during August. By the end of the month, an average coho weighs 15 pounds with plenty going to 17 or 18. Meanwhile, the outstanding spring action never ceases. So August is perhaps the best time of all to take a trophy coho and join the exclusive tyee club for chinooks. Springs are still hanging around when the camp closes at the end of September. The 78-pound camp record for chinook was landed on September 20, 1988.

Sweat was dripping down my backside and my tongue was dangling as, again and again, I led the gorgeous spring alongside the boat – at least half a dozen times. As soon as it spotted the boat's red hull, it tore off with its dorsal fin half out of the water, snaking and shaking its head like a raging bull. Fortunately, just as my energy level coughed and sputtered "empty," Bottay scooped up the bright chrome chinook with another blood-curdling holler. I was almost too pooped and happy to notice.

Back at the camp, we hung our fish on the scale. The accidental salmon that Rick Bourne caught while clearing his line turned out to be a beautiful 12-pound coho, with crimson flash brighter than the primest cut of beef. Wayne's bassin' style chinook tugged the marker to the 26-pound line. My screamer weighed in at just a tad over 28 pounds. But Bob's sagged the pointer all the way down to the 40-pound level.

All in all, I just couldn't help but think that we'd just been through the Langara version of the famous shootout at the OK corral. Or at least the Langara version of the Salmon Lotto. In less than half an hour, we'd caught three springs and one silver – over 100 pounds of Pacific salmon.

Funny thing, though. As we took the grinning pictures of us clutching our prizes, we noticed that the staff smiled politely and said "nice fish," but nobody seemed too impressed. I found out why after dinner, when I had a coffee with the assistant camp manager in his office. John McCullogh pulled out a massive mishmash of the lodge's records.

"Let's look at 1988," he said. "That year, our guests caught more than 3400 springs, and almost half those fish were tyees over 30 pounds."

"What was the biggest?" I asked.

"A chinook that weighed in at 78 pounds," he said.

I gulped at the thought of it.

And 1989 was even better, McCullogh said. "To date, we've caught 4282 chinooks, and 1813 of them were tyees. In fact, six of those springs weighed in at over 70 pounds – the biggest was 76."

Astonishing. If you figure 1,813 tyees in a season for a lodge that holds only 40 anglers at a time, that's one trophy tyee per angler. "And our guests catch far more tyees than cohos," said McCullogh. "Unheard of anywhere else."

Langara's exceptional fishery hinges on several unique factors. First, it's interceptory instead of terminal. Instead of sitting at the estuary of a major salmon river and waiting for fish to return for the spawn, the lodge intercepts them while they frolic out in the ocean. So instead of relying on only one fickle, seasonal source of supply, Langara can tap several. And get first crack at them to boot.

McCullogh says that's he's caught fish that were tagged as far away as California's Sacramento River. And it's common to catch chinook that differ vastly. For instance, some are fish with pug noses from the Columbia River. Or salmon from some B.C. mainland rivers – long, lean, and mean.

"For a week or so," he says, "you might be catching 20 and 25-pounders. Then all of a sudden, big fish show up with totally different physical characteristics."

Another plus for a northern interceptory fishery is that no one source overstays its welcome. So you can't burn out a specific run or stock. Yet with such a variety of strains literally swimming past your door, the odds are good that you're going to rumble with at least one of those genetically diverse marvels that stays in the ocean for an extra year or two of feeding.

The majority of Langara's springs are mature four-year-olds, which explains the lodge's incredible 30-pound average. But plenty of five, six, or seven-year-old fish also cruise around the neighbourhood – those eye-popping 50 to 70 pound monsters.

Langara is almost an embarrassment of fishing riches. When schools of halibut march down the Hecate Strait between the Queen Charlottes and mainland B.C., you can literally catch one on every drift. I asked another guide, Mike Ackert, why anglers at the lodge don't catch more of these superb-tasting flatfish – more than 200 or so a year.

Halibut are too big and too tough, says Ackert. It takes hours and two people to land an 80 or 100-pound fish. And if you don't know what you're doing and you bring the halibut into the boat still green, it can do a lot of damage.

"They're just pure, solid muscle," Ackert added. "Our camp record stands at 114 pounds, but every year we hook much, much bigger halibut."

Langara also has some tremendously underrated bottom fishing for some of the tastiest and most bizarre creatures in the ocean. One afternoon, just for fun, Bob and Wayne and I piled into a boat and scooted over to MacPherson Rock to look for a few of these oddballs. It was foggy mist and choppy, and every once in a while, a wave broke over the stern and soaked our designated driver, Wayne.

We reached the point of MacPherson Rock and began to fuss with our bait. Ever so carefully, we sliced off the heads of our salted herring at the prescribed 45-degree angle, and scooped out the insides to make them twirl. Then we plopped the silvery fish over the side and freespooled them 120 feet down to the bottom.

Bob popped his bait just once. "Got one," he yelled.

"Me too," yelled Wayne.

Then it was my turn: "It's a triple header!" I shouted.

Just what we were catching was often a mystery. Some we knew – big lingcod, yelloweyed rockfish, spiny dogfish sharks, kelp greenling, black rockfish. But when Bob

Getting There

Vancouver International Airport is the arrival and departure point for a trip to Langara Lodge. From there, everything except the price of a fishing licence is part of the package.

The lodge's chartered Convair aircraft lays on a champagne breakfast en route from Vancouver to the tiny hamlet of Sandspit on South Moresby Island. You switch to a helicopter or float plane there for the final leg of the trip.

pulled up a rotund, goldfish-coloured customer with big bulbous eyes and sandpaper scales, and a sharp, spiny dorsal fin, we were at a complete loss.

Bob held the fish at arm's length then tried to shake it loose with a pair of pliers. "What do you think it is?" he said.

"I don't have the foggiest idea," I said. "But man, is it *ugly!*"

Bob started to laugh. Pretty soon, Wayne was laughing too. And from then, the comedy with the uglies built until I had tears running down my cheeks and my sides ached. The climax came when a particularly large wave crashed over Wayne just as a 3-foot shark shook off Bob's hook and joined us in the boat. It skittered around on the floor. Bob and I hopscotched onto the seats. It was the funniest hour of fishing in my life.

And isn't this all a part of a fishing trip to paradise? Lots of laughs and good friends, along with fine accommodation, wonderful food, spectacular country, and the very best salmon fishing in the world?

Two other Langara memories stick in my mind. One was Rick Bourne's comment about breaking the 80-pound salmon barrier. He pointed to some kings that were porpoising and busting a school of needlefish. "There are fish out here," he said, "that send shivers up your spine."

The other memory has to do with something Mike Ackert said about those massive halibut: "Off Coho Point, you find halibut so big you can't even land them. They'll pull your boat around the ocean until you cut them off."

Talk about the stuff of dreams.

Langara Fishing Lodge Ltd.
436 West Second Ave.
Vancouver, B.C. V5Y 1E2.
Phone: 604-873-4228

Getting There

It's fishing in luxury – dinner with wine, box lunches, a bottomless supply of hot drinks, soft drinks, fruit, candy bars, and a Lucas rescue boat that stops by your fishing boat from time to time to restock your food and drink. The lodge supplies all rods, reels, tackle, bait, raincoats, slickers, and rubber boots. You hang the rainwear in a special drying room and it's all warm as toast when you head out again. Bring along long johns, warm shirts, one or two wool sweaters, rugged pants, a toque, and a pair of finger gloves. And don't forget a camera and plenty of film.

Yelloweyed Rockfish

SALTWATER BOTTOMFISH

WHAT KIND OF FISH *IS* THAT?

When you go fishing off Canada's west coast, you never know what you're going to catch!

Quite a few years ago I saved up a little money, quit my job, and moved out to a little place called Point Holmes, on Vancouver Island. I wanted to be a writer, so I resolved to spend five months doing nothing but writing, mailing stories out for publication, and at the end of the winter I'd see whether my bank balance had moved into the black or the red.

The little house on Point Holmes rented out for $125 per month. There was a lumpy fireplace of river rock, a backyard with wind-warped evergreens, and a long grassy slope leading down to the beach. Sitting at the window in the living-room, I'd peck away at an old Underwood and try to ignore the never-ending passion play of nature enacted outside. Imagine the scene: a distant cordillera of snow-capped coastal mountains, a twenty-mile wide stretch of ocean, whales, seals, and salmon rolling in the offshore swell; then closer, crows and eagles bickering on the beach. Ducks whirling past. One morning a ten-point buck deer, for no reason whatsoever beyond sheer exuberance at being alive, came sprinting down the beach, running in water that was just deep enough to create an incredible commotion of spray. Sometimes the choice was simple: draw the curtain or give up. Shut off the typewriter. Go fishing.

Usually I could resist the urge until about four o'clock in the afternoon. But five minutes later, I'd be dragging the canoe across the beach, launching it in the mild surf, and paddling out in search of dinner. In British Columbia, the most popular fish is the salmon. To fish for salmon, anglers use big boats and trolling rods. Sitting in their swivel chairs, they listen to the natter of their outboard motors and wait for a salmon to hit their trolled bait. Since I was poor, ill-equipped, and uninformed on such matters, I went out bottom-fishing in my humble canoe. And I don't know if I'll ever have such a good time again.

> **"Bottomfish" is a catch-all term attached to a broad variety of saltwater species that hang around rocks, reefs and the ocean bottom. Many are bass-like in appearance, and it's usually safe to refer to these as "rockfish."**

The water in the Strait of Georgia is turquoise green and so clear you can see pebbles and starfish on the bottom at 50 feet. In those days, I had a hunch that fish wouldn't bite if you could see them. So I'd paddle the canoe out to the deeper water, where the low afternoon sun slanted in golden lines down into the purple depths, and drop my Buzz Bomb over the side. The Buzz Bomb is a great all-around lure, appealing to many species of fish, and it would seldom take very much bottom-bouncing before I'd feel a solid thump and my spinning reel would begin to whir and chatter as a stubborn bottomfish ran away with the line. Pumping, I'd raise the fish until it blew its top and took off for the bottom again. Eventually, the creature would loom into visibility, magnified and distorted by the blurring panes of green water. Often, my first response would be a long pause, "What the hell kind of fish is that?"

Bottomfish is a catch-all term attached to a broad variety of saltwater species that hang around rocks, reefs, and the ocean bottom. Many are bass-like in appearance, and it's usually, but not always, safe to refer to these as "rockfish." Sometimes rockfish are orange, sometimes they're black. Sometimes they have bug-eyes, radiant quills, and bulldog teeth. One bottom fish has a warty head and a dazed, cross-eyed expression. I believe this species is called the "Irish Lord" but I'm not sure. Neither is anyone else. One of the nice things about bottomfishing is that you're an explorer, a collector of unknown specimens. Unless you're a zoologist, you're bound to catch an occasional fish that you'll have trouble identifying without a textbook.

Most of Canada's saltwater bottomfish share one quality: they are absolutely delicious. Even the small shark you often catch in B.C. waters called the Spiny Dogfish is good eating. Most English fish and chips are made from dogfish. After a few hours of Buzz-Bombing I'd usually have the makings of a great dinner, plus enough left over for lunch the next day. Paddling home, I'd watch the orange sky turn violet above the mountains.

That was quite a few years ago, and I'm still working as a writer. As fate would have it, after five months I had a little more money than I started with. So I decided to go on to bigger and better things. Now I spend a lot of time in a city, staring at a computer while a phone rings in the background. But I often wonder: What if I had added up my cash and found that I had exactly the same amount I started with? What if I'd stayed there forever? Typing in the morning, fishing in the evening, living in that little house by the ocean. Would they call that success?

The Buzz Bomb

Back in the 1970s a friend of mine came out to Northwestern Ontario to try a little freshwater walleye and pike fishing. Ted lives in Comox, British Columbia, where you can go downhill skiing and salmon fishing in the same morning, and never drive further than 15 miles from your front door. So Ted has fairly picky ideas about what constitutes entertainment.

On a really good day, it's pretty hard to compete with west coast fishing. And we weren't having a good day. It was hot and quiet, and after two hours of casting we hadn't caught a thing. Ted was beginning to mumble nostalgically about the muscle-bound rockfish you can catch, one after another, around Hornby Island. And when he pulled out a saltwater lure and began tying it onto his line I couldn't keep quiet any longer. "Ted, that is the ugliest, dumbest, most useless-looking lure I've ever seen."

"They work great out on the west coast."

"Well, we're not on the west coast."

Ted didn't say anything. Nothing is more annoying than somebody being diplomatic when you're trying to have an argument. Ted casted the silly-looking chunk of metal into the water and immediately hooked a fat, golden walleye. I netted the fish and before I could get my line back in the water he was into another

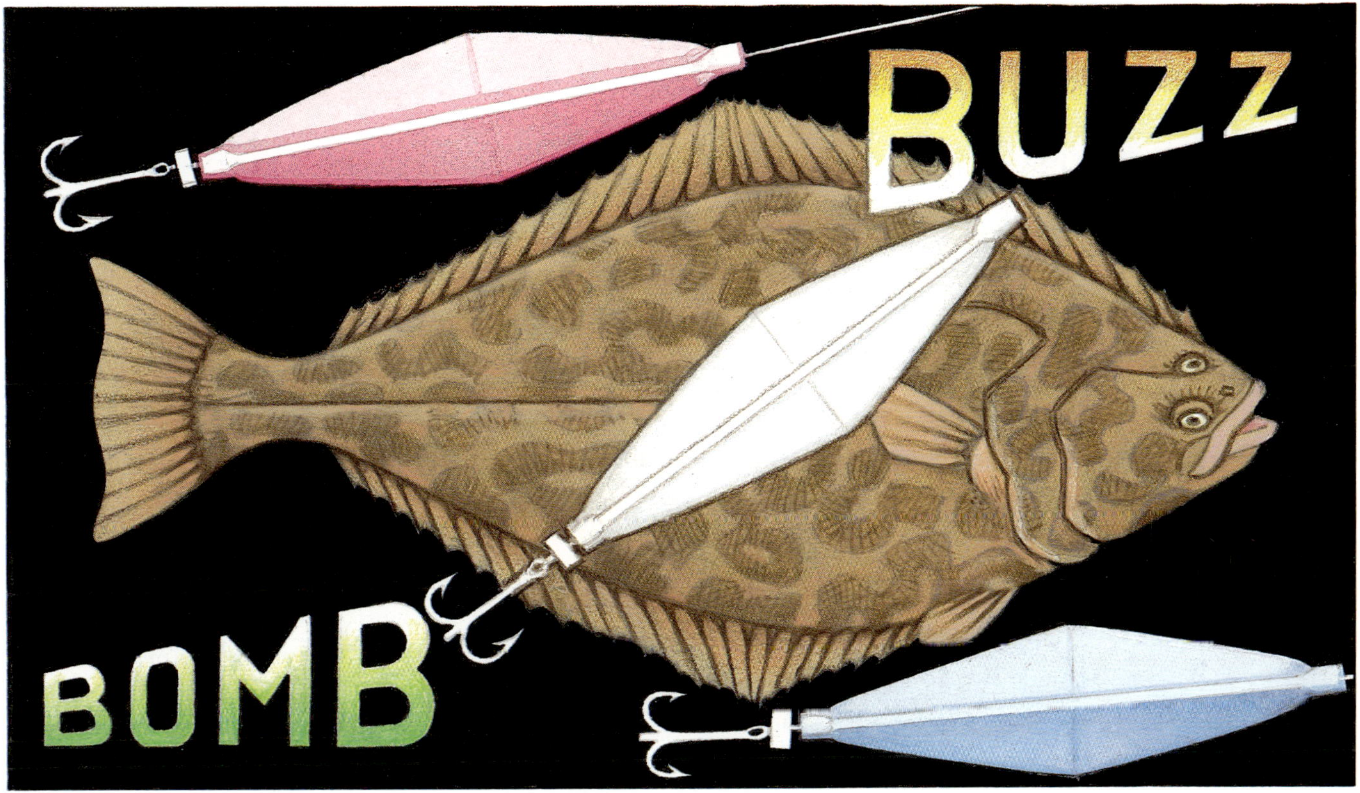

Buzz Bomb with Halibut

one. In the next twenty minutes he caught three walleyes and four northern pikes. I finally swallowed my pride. "May I have a look at that lure, old buddy?"

Ted's lure was about the size and shape of a little pocket knife. It had flat sides and was pointed at both ends. It looked more like a chisel than a fishing lure. But when you dropped it in the water, it fluttered and flashed like an injured minnow. Ted tossed me one. "It's called a Buzz Bomb," he said. "A guy just down the street from where I live invented it."

Since that day, I've caught everything from walleye to salmon to red snapper on Buzz Bombs, and once, for a few moments, I even hooked a big Pacific sailfish with a Buzz Bomb the size of my baby finger. The lure was invented by a man named Rex Field, who, according to unofficial angling history, stood on the Comox Pier one day, watching salmon feed on schools of herring. Field noticed that a big school could swim past the salmon unmolested, but whenever a sick herring fluttered away from the main school, it was attacked immediately. Injured baitfish swim differently from healthy individuals, and most lures tend to imitate the latter. Rex Field theorized that the vibrations sent off by an injured fish attract predators, and he tried building a lure that fluttered awkwardly in the same way. The Comox pier was well lit at night, and usually hosted a good population of baitfish and predators, so he used the site for his lure trials. To test whether the fish were attracted to the appearance or the sound of his lure, he suspended a curtain of plastic from a two-by-four, and let his portable lab float in the water.

Rex Field ascertained that fish would home in on a vibrating lure even when it was concealed behind a curtain, so he reasoned that sound was as important as visual cues in attracting fish. The result of repeated trials was the Buzz Bomb, and its effectiveness was proven, to me at least, that hot day in northwestern Ontario fifteen years ago. Over thousands of hours, Rex Field and his son Doug researched and refined the Buzz Bomb concept, adding innovations like the use of a special alloy that makes a ringing noise when tapped, and transmits sound about 75 times further than other metals. Now, anglers all up and down the west coast use them, and you'd be hard-pressed to find a good tackle store that doesn't have Buzz Bombs on the rack. Although it hasn't been around as long as the Five of Diamonds or the Gibbs spoon, the Buzz Bomb is gradually becoming a classic.

For bottom fish like halibut, rockfish, lingcod, and other species that hang around underwater structure and wait for food to come to them, the best way to use the Buzz Bomb is to lower it to the bottom and then jig it gently up and down. On the up stroke, the Buzz Bomb swims like a healthy baitfish. On the release, it flutters downward like a crippled minnow. Doug Field says that women and children are often the most successful users of the Buzz Bomb, because they are not overly aggressive in jerking it up and down. Field says that a very gentle stroke is required. "Stand up," he says. "And keep that Buzz Bomb coming up and buzzing down, lift slow, drop fast, lift slow, drop fast, and so on. When a fish grabs it, set the hook."

For wide-roaming fish like salmon, bonito, dorado, and other predatory species, the Buzz Bomb works well as a casting lure. In the Mexican Pacific, I use Buzz Bombs almost exclusively for casting around reefs and tidal rips. A relatively rapid retrieval seems to work the best, sweeping the lure in, letting it drop, sweeping it in, letting it drop, and so on. When a big needlefish or sierra hits the Buzz Bomb, you don't have to worry about setting the hook. Saltwater fish strike a Buzz Bomb so hard you'll feel like you caught the bumper of an accelerating pickup truck.

Buzz Bomb Lure Corporation,
2498 Cousins Avenue
Courtney B.C. V9N 7T5
Phone: 604-338-5364, FAX 604-338-1220

Photo courtesy
Aikens Lake
Wilderness Lodge

FAMILY FISHING RESORTS

It's a rule of thumb that the best places to fish in Canada aren't accessible by road. There are exceptions, of course – the Red River, for example – but light angling pressure and pristine habitat often add up to good fishing.

Road-accessible resorts with excellent service, nice scenery, and abundant populations of gamefish are not as common as fly-in resorts with the same characteristics. And if you're looking for a place that has lots of fish and is inexpensive, the search gets narrower still.

But patrons of road-accessible, family resorts are not just interested in top-notch fishing. In general, experienced anglers with high ambitions head for the back country. But those of us with families, pets and relatives tend to prefer the drive-in lodges. In a more civilized setting, children, old folks, and non-anglers can always find something to do on a rainy day. Most drive-in resorts have golf, tennis, horseback riding and other activities in the neighbourhood. Swimming beaches, handicraft shops, and easy chairs down by the water provide relaxation for less athletic types. In summary, a drive-in family resort may not be the best place in the world to go looking for the next world-record salmon or lake trout, but it will be a much better place to take the kids, the dog, a chubby suspense novel, and a couple of fishing poles.

Family vacation spots fall into a number of general categories. Starting with the least expensive, these are:

1. **Unserviced campgrounds**. These range from tenting sites way off in the bush somewhere to government-maintained campgrounds alongside roads and hiking trails. Advantages are low expense, few people, much wildlife, and good fishing. Disadvantages are lack of amenities, lots of chores, cooking, cleaning, erecting tents, etc., and the necessity of purchasing a great deal of camping equipment. A canoe alone, for example, might cost $1000. Unless you plan to do a lot of camping, you may find it cheaper to book a suite at a 5-star hotel.
2. **Serviced campgrounds**. For vacationers travelling with kids and all the paraphernalia that entails, a serviced campground is often an ideal choice. Showers, bathrooms, drinking water, and electricity provide a basic level of creature comfort, and there are usually playgrounds, swimming beaches, boat rentals, and other diversions for kids in the neighbourhood. Since many of the basics, like boats, electricity, and road access are provided, serviced campgrounds are often a less cumbersome proposition than wilderness campsites. On the down side, serviced campgrounds are not usually located next to red-hot fishing spots, and they often lack privacy. But these may not be top priorities when you're looking for a few days of swimming, bonfires, and fun-fishing with the kids.
3. **Light Housekeeping Resorts**. These are one step above serviced campgrounds, in the sense that they provide a roof over your head. All you need to bring are your groceries and toothbrush. Light housekeeping resorts are of course more expensive than serviced campgrounds, but they usually offer more comfort and privacy for your money. The best light

housekeeping resorts are usually booked well ahead of time, so it's not always easy to find a good light housekeeping cabin on short notice.

4. **American Plan Resorts**. The Cadillac of vacation options American Plan resorts, which offer a completely catered vacation. Meals, accommodation, and sometimes even guided fishing trips are included in the price. The quality of the fishing may be no better than at light housekeeping resorts, but the luxurious surroundings make these places popular with couples, honeymooners, and others who are interested in a hassle-free, first-class holiday.

The following selection of family resorts represents all these options: They offer unusually good fishing, beautiful scenery, and friendly, professional staffing, all at a good price. They are organized along an imaginary route running from east to west across western Canada. A good tourist approach might be to set out by automobile and spend a couple of days visiting each one of them.

Laughing Waters Lodge

Laughing Waters Lodge
Barb & Rob Madden
P.O. Box 7
Sioux Narrows, Ontario

The Lake of the Woods district in Northwestern Ontario is a beautiful wilderness realm of lakes and forest and pine-feathered islands.

Laughing Waters Lodge, just a few miles north of Sioux Narrows, is a light housekeeping resort that has many attractions for children, including a sand beach, a diving float, a playground, and so on. And it's situated in a part of the lake that has excellent fishing for walleye, muskie, and bass.

The cabins are log, very pretty, with screened verandas, painted floors, and that rustic, rickety ambience that we associate with quaint old resorts. It's owned by Rob and Barb Madden, two refugees from Toronto. They left because they couldn't stand the lifestyle. "Lineups," says Rob Madden. "That's what I remember the most. Lineups on the freeway. Lineups at the grocery store. Lineups at the bank. I spent about two hours every day looking at somebody's back."

Barb and Rob taught school in the Lake of the Woods area, and fell in love with it. "The clean air, the space. When we left to go back to Toronto, we told some friends to keep an eye open for us, for a nice resort or lodge. Maybe if we found the right place, we'd buy it."

Like many real-estate shoppers the Maddens were naïve, and tied the move to a number of precise conditions. The place had to be pretty but not too expensive, rustic but not too primitive, winterized, accessible by road, located on the water, and have a good chunk of undeveloped property attached. "And we also wanted teaching jobs in the area. And a nice sand beach." The Lake of the Woods is sparsely settled, and there are not many resorts to choose from. Most are family businesses that seldom come up on the market, so the odds of finding one that matched their expectations were slim.

One spring day their friends telephoned. They had found it.

"I flew up and took a look at the place. It was April. The snow was all gone and the lake was frozen. It was sunny and hot. The country was empty. And life was beginning again. It's my favourite time of the year. The real estate agents and the owners gave me a full tour of the lodge. It was a gorgeous, 3200-foot, log-beamed house with an enormous fieldstone fireplace. There were six cabins on the property. It was all surrounded by cathedral pines, right on the lake. It had everything we wanted, the good all-weather road, the nearby school with the possibility of teaching jobs. And it was in our price range. It even had a sand beach.

Rob Madden sat by himself in the lodge for two hours, looking out at the lake. He got up and telephoned Barb. "I think this is it."

Today, Laughing Waters Lodge offers fine lodging and great swimming. There's a wonderful, tree-shaded sand beach with a diving platform, well protected from boat traffic and big waves. For the kids, there's a playground with teeter-totter and other diversions. The lease expensive cabins rent for $490 per week, or $196 per weekend, and fishing boats are available at $55 per day. "Many people just rent one of the canoes for $20 per day," says Barb. "There's excellent fishing for bass at Berry Creek, just five minutes' paddle from here. Or you can go casting for northerns at Flatrock Point close by. Everybody catches fish. The guests like to bring home a couple for supper and release the rest."

Every Wednesday there's a Campfire Night where Rob plays the guitar and guests produce anything from spoons to bagpipes. Hotdogs broil on the grill. And sparks fly up into the darkness. Laughing Waters Lodge is a rare place that offers something for everybody.

Gunn Lake Lodge

Gunn Lake Lodge
Sally Kendall and
Kelly Gibson
Minaki, Ontario
P0X 1J0
Ph: 807-224-2321

Still in Northwestern Ontario, albeit two hour's drive west of Laughing Waters Lodge, perched up on a high cliff above the sparkling blue water of Gunn Lake, sits a little hamlet of handsome cedar cottages called Gunn Lake Lodge.

Unlike most wilderness resorts, Gunn Lake Lodge stays open year-round, and does a good business in the wintertime hosting honeymooners, anglers, business conferences, cross-country skiers, and couples seeking a romantic weekend getaway. Gunn Lake Lodge is an American Plan resort, and along with boats, canoes, hiking trails, sauna, and hot tub, it has what many visitors and locals consider to be the best dining for a hundred miles around.

Located on the productive Winnipeg River system, Gunn Lake Lodge has immediate boat access to hundreds of miles of wilderness shoreline, lakes, islands, channels, and good gamefish habitat. Fishing pressure is fairly steady, but the Winnipeg River still succeeds at producing many large walleye, pike, and muskellunge. Every year, guests at Gunn Lake Lodge catch walleye over 10 pounds, pike over 20 pounds, and muskellunge over 30. Fish of that size class demand time and effort, however, and most anglers content themselves with catching a few walleye and then going ashore on some secluded island and watching their guide prepare a delicious lunch over an open fire.

Gunn Lake Lodge is owned by Sally Kendall and Kelly Gibson. Kelly is a big, curly-haired ex-hockey player. After working for years as a lumberjack, building contractor, and canoe outfitter, he started Gunn Lake Lodge in partnership with Sally Kendall, an American ex-patriate who cut her teeth in the hospitality biz working as a hat-check girl at her father's steak house in Illinois. Gunn Lake Lodge has good fishing, but it's not just a fishing lodge. There's a Chicago Jazz festival every summer, many companies hold working conferences there, and most visitors come to just relax, soak in the hot tub under a starry sky, and of course enjoy the top-notch cuisine, which by my understanding differs from food in the sense that it comes with a detailed and formalized introduction from your bow-tie-wearing waiter.

Best time to fish at Gunn Lake is autumn. September is turn-over time, and for a few weeks the weather is grey and stormy. Then the summer air mass seems to get used to the idea that it has lost the battle for another year and things settle down. The sky clears. The frost-nipped leaves turn golden on the hills and the water takes on its richest hue of cobalt. That's the time that Winnipeg River fishing hits a peak. Few baitfish are left from the summer's production and the walleye, pike, and muskie are hungry and on-the-hunt. Through the long period of pleasant sunny autumn days in October anglers often have the river to themselves – everyone else has quit for the season – and the scenery is at its finest. I remember a day several years ago when I went fishing with Sally Kendall. The leaves were down and the woods seemed stripped and bare, waiting silently for what was to come. We left Gunn Lake Lodge and motored across a glassy lake, dark as slate under a sky that looked an awful lot like winter. Yet it was a warm evening and so quiet that you could hear people talking a mile away. We killed the motor and drifted up to a spot where I'd done very well the day before, squiring some of Sally's guests. I occasionally guide anglers out of Gunn Lake Lodge. Rigging up with tiny jigs and live minnows, we casted up towards the shore. On every third or fourth cast, we'd feel a heavy strike and the fight would be on. After a struggle of several minutes, the fish would come to net: walleye of shining gold, 4 pounds and larger. Fish so beautiful it made our hearts ache just to look at them.

After an hour of this, whispering as the fish came in, "Oh god, look at this one," we began to feel guilty, so we stowed our rods and left the walleye in peace.

Motoring down to the south end of Gunn Lake, we went ashore on a smooth hump of mossy granite. Building a fire of weathered driftwood, we watched sparks whirl up into the dark sky. The frigid lake water did a good job of cooling our white wine, as I cleaned two of our prettiest walleyes for supper. Soon we were eating a delicious meal in a scene of such primitivism and shadowy, fire-lit beauty that we felt like pinching each other to see if we were dreaming.

Gunn Lake Lodge is often booked solid, so it's a good idea to plan your visit well ahead of time. If you need a guide, ask Sally for me. I can set you up with someone, either myself, or if I'm busy, one of the good local guides. She'll know where to find me. She's my wife.

Inverness Falls Resort

Stu Cornell's father was in the tourist business, operating a fishing lodge, and so was his grandfather, and so is Stu himself. Over three generations, a lot of things have remained constant in the backwoods resort business.

People still gravitate to the Canadian wilderness to enjoy the fresh air and the scenery and to catch a few fish. Loons still sound the same, their calls echoing over a glassy lake at sundown, and fresh walleye, beans, bacon, and onions still smell as delicious, popping and sizzling over a fire of driftwood.

After guiding fishermen for eleven years at his father's fishing lodge, fixing motors, cleaning fish, and hanging out with the guys, Stu Cornell could easily have glided into the traditional fishing lodge business. But instead, he and his sweetheart Judy took off and ran remote Hudson's Bay Company trading posts in the Canadian arctic. The experience taught them more than they already knew about nature, which was quite a lot. When they came back down south, they started a little tourist camp. They committed themselves to running a resort that was environmentally smart, comfortable, nature-oriented, and that appealed to people of all backgrounds. They wanted to run a place where a single mother could take her son fishing. Or where a couple could enjoy the ultimate honeymoon. "I've seen too many cut-and-run style fishing lodges," Stu says. "Operators go into a lake, throw up a few plywood cabins, and strip-mine all the fish in a couple of years. I wanted to try a different approach, or stay out of the tourist business altogether."

Inverness Falls Resort
Rennie, Manitoba
R0E 1R0
Phone:
204-369-5336

Inverness Falls Resort

The result is Inverness Falls Resort. Located on a pretty lake 85 miles east of Winnipeg, the Cornells' place consists of a variety of nicely-appointed cabins in a wooded setting. Hot tubs, saunas, canoes, row boats, mountain bikes, and other features provide diversion for guests in the summer. In winter, cross-country skiing, ice-fishing, wood-burning fireplaces, and, of course, the hot tub and sauna offer a weekend alternative to the cold and dismal city. Brereton Lake, with an average depth of 16 feet, is a fertile lake with an irregular shoreline, lots of bottom structure and baitfish, so it is an ideal environment for northern pike and walleye. The Rennie River tumbles over a falls right in the middle of the property, then winds through a forest, past the cabins, and it too is a good place to fish. Brereton Lake is accessible by road and there are cottages nearby, but the lake's fertility provides a higher quality of fishing than is found in most drive-in lakes.

The real icing on the cake is the remote log cabin that the Cornells maintain at nearby War Eagle Lake. All of us sometimes entertain fantasies of how we'd rebuild civilization if we could just start from scratch, and perhaps there was more than a little of that daydreaming behind the Cornells' wilderness retreat at War Eagle. You can't drive to War Eagle. You have to hike in over a three-and-a-half-mile trail. Or, if you have little children or a bum knee or you're just a bit too old, you can catch a ride with Stu in his track truck, a sleek and futuristic-looking six-passenger van that goes anywhere. Once you arrive, Stu gives what he calls his rules and then, with a gallant wave, he disappears. What follows is utter peace. No traffic. No neighbours. No problems. Just kerosene lamps, a wood stove, a solar-powered hand-made log palace, and a virginal wilderness lake.

"I had a lot of trouble getting permission to put a cabin on War Eagle," Stu says. "The government was reluctant, because it's a provincial park. But I convinced them that it was going to be a different kind of outpost camp. We try to have a zero-impact on the local environment. It may seem a little primitive at first, cooking dinner on the old wood stove and reading in bed by the light of an oil lamp, but after people have been there for a few days, it starts to get in their blood."

Stu hired two rough-neck Scottish log builders to help him construct War Eagle retreat. "I thought I was a bit of a fanatic, on this business of wilderness purism," he says. "But the first day of work I showed up with my Skil saw and all my power tools and they pointed to them and said, 'What's that junk for? We don't use power. We build by hand.' " Throughout the winter, as snow howled through the trees, they shared a tent. Three men crowded in together, doing a job for a lot of pride and very little money. Cornell says that it took three times longer, by the Scotsmen's methods, but the process left him with a renewed belief in quality workmanship. "It took this fellow all morning to mount a single log," he says. "He handed me the saw and said, 'Go ahead, make the window opening.' But I couldn't do it. It was like cutting into a work of art."

Stu stocked the lake with smallmouth bass and the bass have thrived. They share the lake with a population of 2 to 5 pound northern pike. He has divided the lake into zones where you can fish for supper and others where you can fish on a catch-and-release basis. "In case it's a windy day, this strategy provides good places where you can fish off the shore. So there is always good fishing no matter what the weather. Also, we don't allow fishing off the dock right in front of the cabin, because we want people to be able to swim without worrying about snagged fishhooks." For emergencies, or problems of any kind, the cabin has a solar-powered telephone. "I like to talk to the guests, if they feel like calling every day," Stu says. "It's fun to find out how they're doing."

The Cornells generally advise people to keep their groups to six or under for War Eagle Lake. "Four is good," Stu says. "But two is even better. Three days is about the length of an ideal stay. If you go in for three days, you'll catch lots of fish, have a wonderful rest, and I guarantee you'll be reluctant to leave when I return."

A CABIN IN THE WOODS

Riding Mountain is a heavily wooded ridge that rises thousands of feet above the surrounding Manitoba prairie. Along the southern edge of Riding Mountain National Park is The Trailhead Cabin. Very private, with excellent American meals available, the Trailhead is an excellent, rustic place to hole up for a couple of days or more and explore the local blue-water mountain lakes for the various species of trout that abound there.

The Trailhead Cabin itself is a spacious, open-area log building nestled in the forest of Wasamin Creek. Wildlife like elk, coyotes, deer, and moose abound in the nearby woods. Besides fishing, visitors can go horseback riding, swimming, and hiking in the fabulous back country of the Park. As an interesting sideline, you can also sign up for painting or drawing lessons while you're there. Anne Schuster, your host, is an accomplished artist. Open year-round. You can contact Anne Schuster by writing to her at Box 14, Lake Audy, Manitoba, R0J 0Z0 or by phoning 204-848-7649.

Camping in MANITOBA

North from Winnipeg, Highway 6 runs straight as a knife-cut into the deep forests that cover the top two-thirds of the province. The highway is so flat and flawless that, with the sun pouring down and the spruce forest scrolling endlessly past, you find yourself either nodding off or trying to resist the urge to nail the gas pedal to the floor.

One time a big timber wolf sashayed out onto the pavement ahead just as my speedo needle edged past 100 mph. I tapped the brake and a half-second later a Royal Canadian Mountie came over the hill. The wolf spurted into the bush and the Mountie flipped on his lights. "I'm going fishing," I said. "Can't you just give me a warning?"

"Give you a warning?" he laughed. "If I'd clocked you three miles per hour faster I'd have had to put you in jail."

Courtesy of Mr. Wolf, I arrived at Paint Lake Provincial Recreation Area a few hours later. First stop, Pisew Falls, tallest waterfall in Manitoba, where the Grass River catapults over a long dizzy series of rock staircases into a canyon of mist and sun-lanced rainbow. Kneeling down on the funky-smelling gravel below the falls, you can splash cold water on your face and shake off the numbness of that long drive. Paint Lake Campground has 94 unserviced sites, barbecue pits, boat rental and launch, and a playground. In the immediate area are many lakes and rivers with absolutely outstanding world-class fishing. Very large northern pike, abundant walleye, big lake trout. On a June night, dusk doesn't set in until eleven in the evening. By three a.m., it's morning again.

Paint Lake Provincial Campground
Phone: 1-800-665-0040

Camping in SASKATCHEWAN

Ninety miles north of Prince Albert, Saskatchewan, are the Gem Lakes, a chain of pretty, small lakes stocked with a variety of hungry trout. Rainbow trout, brown trout, brook trout, and lake trout offer abundant action for anglers who want an inexpensive but high quality camping vacation.

Jade Lake is as green as a jewel, and supports a healthy population of splake, lake trout, and rainbows. Opal Lake is a narrow, evergreen-rimmed lake with brookies and rainbows. Sapphire Lake is long and narrow, well-sheltered from wind, and harbours a good population of splake. Using a canoe or belly boat, anglers can drift the quiet waters of any of these lakes, presenting nymphs or leech imitations with a fly rod, or tiny spoons with a spinning rod. Some anglers find good success with a small jig tipped with a live leech. For kids, a worm and bobber combination is foolproof.

The two best campgrounds are located at Little Bear Lake and at Piprell Lake. The Little Bear Campground is slightly more modern, with twelve electric sites, shower, beach, boat launch, and dumping station for RV campers. The Piprell Lake Campground has 23 non-electric campsites, with beach, boat rental, shower and laundry facilities.

Gwen Hoodle
Piprell Lake Campground
Box 40
Meath Park, Saskatchewan S0J 1T0
Mobile: 306-YL3-2047

Bob Ackerman
Little Bear Campground
Mile 62, Hanson Lake Rd., via Prince Albert, Saskatchewan S6V 5Z5
Phone: 306-426-2280

Camping in ALBERTA

In northern Alberta, Lesser Slave Lake is a huge natural body of water with abundant populations of walleye, pike and whitefish. The best way to fish Lesser Slave inexpensively is to camp at Shaw's Point Resort, a 60-site serviced campground with laundry, store, marina, boat rentals, and kids' playground. Less expensive, more secluded unserviced camp sites are also available. Nearby, there's a mile-long white sand beach for swimming.

Shaw's Point Lakeside Resort
PO Box 1161
High Prairie, Alberta T0G 1E0
Phone: 403-751-3900

LIGHT TEEPEE-KEEPING IN ALBERTA

One of the most original light housekeeping resorts in Alberta actually features painted teepees instead of cabins. Located in the Kananaskis valley, Sundance Lodges has good fishing nearby for bull trout and brown trout in the Kananaskis River, and there's also horseback riding, hiking, golfing, and cycling in the area.

The teepees have wooden floors, bed frames and mattresses, fire pits, picnic tables, and lanterns. The first things you become aware of in the morning are sunlight streaming through canvas, bird calls, and the scent of coffee drifting on the sharp mountain air. "It can be 80 above outside," says Sheryl Green, who operates Sundance Lodges with her husband Brian, "but it's always cool in a teepee." There are hot showers on the property and modern washrooms. You can rent campfire cooking kits, towels, and bedding.

Sundance Lodges
Box 190
Kananaskis Village, Alberta T0L 2H0
Phone: 403-591-7122

Camping in BRITISH COLUMBIA

The Okanagan Valley is one of the most popular places in Canada to retire. Located in the British Columbia Interior, the valley runs in a north-south direction between two mountain ranges. The weather is hot, sunny, and dry. The Okanagan gets 2000 hours of sunshine a year – more than Hawaii. And the summer water temperature in Osoyoos Lake averages 75°F, which is about the same temperature as the water along the Pacific beaches of southern Mexico.

Osoyoos Lake is a picturesque, turquoise lake at the south end of the Okanagan Valley. Surrounded by mountains, Osoyoos Lake has 2000 feet of fine sand beach next to the campground at the base of Mount Baldy. Fishing is available in most of the nearby lakes. Rainbow trout and kokanee are the main species. The ideal way to fish the area is with a canoe that's small enough to strap to the roof of your vehicle. Ideal time is June, before vacation time. Around that time, the lakes are full of hungry rainbow trout.

The campground has 85 serviced sites with laundry, boat ramp, volleyball, horseshoes, campfires, and recreational activities for children.

Brookvale Holiday Campground
1219 45th Street
Osoyoos, B.C. V0H 1V0
Phone: 604-495-7514

Resorts in BRITISH COLUMBIA

The Kamloops Region is a great area for trout fishing, with over 200 lakes within a 25-mile radius of the city. In June, 1993, three of these lakes – Roche, Tunkwa and Edith – were considered important enough trout producers to be chosen as host locations for the 123rd Annual World Fly Fishing Championship.

Near Kamloops there are many excellent lodges with campgrounds, light housekeeping, and American plan options for families. Most of these have activities like horseback riding, sailboarding, canoeing, biking, and kayaking to go along with the fishing. One unusual activity available in BC resort country is gold-panning in mountain streams. Although gold nuggets are rare, kids enjoy panning for the water-polished agates and pebbles that are common in stream beds.

Roche Lake Lodge was one of the hosts for the international fly fishing competition. Roche Lake's American Plan includes meals, accommodation, and a boat. The lodge has a conference centre, a Jacuzzi, swimming pool, dining-room, and many extras like mountain bikes, bonfires, and canoes. There are also two chalets with kitchenettes for those who prefer light housekeeping.

Caverhill Lodge is a secluded, full American Plan resort with room for eighteen guests in private cabins. Guests spin or fly fish for trout on eighteen lakes, each of which has boats on site. Guests are served three meals per day.

Tunkwa Lake Resort is open year-round, with both camping and light housekeeping cottages available. The lodge has a Finnish sauna, child care on site, fireplaces, showers and full plumbing, and a nearby lake with trout that run up to 10 pounds.

Roche Lake Resort
Box 669
Kamloops, B.C.
V2C 5L7
Ph: 604-828-2007

Caverhill Lodge
Box 190
Barriere, B.C.
V0E 1E0
Ph: 604-372-6193

Tunkwa Lake Resort
Box 196
Logan Lake, B.C.
V0K 1W0
Ph: 604-523-9697

Preparing a shore lunch

EATING THEM

A Fishing Guide Reveals the Forbidden Secrets of Shore Lunch

Many years ago I guided a couple of Green Berets on a fishing trip into the Canadian woods. Bob and Kenton had spent two years in the Central Highlands of Vietnam, doing long-range recon patrols with Montagnard tribesmen, sleeping on the ground, eating the odd snake, and generally receiving a fairly good schooling in the basics of wilderness cuisine.

All morning I looked forward to our shore lunch, when I hoped these two bush professionals would teach me some of their secret, last-ditch methods of wilderness cooking, such as fire-making by rubbing sticks, baking with wet mud, or pounding root fibres into pancake flour. But at lunch they seemed confused. "I can't get the fire going," Bob apologized. "Do you have a lighter?" In the middle of showing Bob how to light a fire I was obliged to rescue Kenton, who had a jumbo can of beans clamped between his knees, and was sawing at it avidly with a large, dangerous-looking knife.

Cooking shore lunch doesn't require the ingenuity of an artist, but it's always a bit of a trick. Not only do you have to prepare food over an open fire, but you have to catch it first. Shore lunch is a long-standing tradition at Canadian wilderness lodges, and it's one of those half-mysterious feats that, once learned, scores major points with wife, family, relatives, and others who can't be bothered catching fish, but are quite willing to eat them. As in a stage play, the first prerequisite of shore lunch is the Setting. Visualize a wilderness island in mid-summer, sea gulls drifting on the water, boats pulled up on the shore, tourists standing around a campfire from which white smoke is unfurling, and a weathered, silent, somewhat dour-looking fishing guide kneeling by the fire. Deftly shifting a frying pan in his gloved hands, the guide/chef dishes out a plate of mysterious foodstuffs to his guests, who nibble tentatively, then smile in delight. "Man, this isn't bad," says one. "Not bad? Are you kidding?" remarks another. "This is the best meal I've had in years." A third tourist casts an admiring eye at the guide. "Walleye Johnny," declares a third, "you oughta start your own restaurant in New York City."

What's the recipe? Fishing guides don't like giving away their trade secrets, and if you are fishing at a full-service American Plan lodge, the preparations for shore lunch will be your guide's problem, not yours. But with the economic restraints of the last few years, many anglers are patronizing Canada's less-expensive light housekeeping resorts, where tourists and anglers rent a cabin with kitchen and perhaps a boat, but supply their own groceries, equipment, and dishing expertise. At light housekeeping resorts, there's no guide to slave over a fire and hand you a plate brimming with delicious fish, corn, and potatoes after a successful morning's fishing trip. Instead, patrons of Light Housekeeping resorts often pack sandwiches, which are a poor second-best to a hot meal cooked on an open fire. If you're planning a trip to a northern resort this year, and won't be using the services of a fishing guide, why not cook your own shore lunch? There's no better way to win the undying admiration of your fishing buddies, provided you don't get sand in the fish or light the island on fire.

Cooking the meal itself is largely a matter of pre-planning, and every fishing guide, no matter how experienced, is thrown into a state of panic if he misplaces the most important item: the **shore lunch list**. The list describes what's needed when you're cooking lunch 40 minutes' boat ride from the nearest kitchen, and since the list, like shore lunch itself, is reduced to the basics, missing a single item can be disastrous. Tourists who've travelled a thousand miles and shelled out as many dollars to go fishing in the Canadian wilderness expect a certain level of expertise, and guides have recurrent nightmares about forgetting to bring some crucial item. In this case, you are the guide, and if you want to avoid being made the butt of your comrades' bar-room humour for weeks after the fishing trip is over, don't try making shore lunch without bringing plates, cooking oil, or worse yet, matches.

Anglers who would like to put on an occasional backwoods shore lunch for fishing buddies or family should make several copies of their list and conceal them in various places around the building. I keep one taped to the inside of the shore lunch box, one in the fridge, and another someplace I can't remember.

Shore Lunch List *(based on 4 people)*

- ✓ 5 plates
- ✓ silverware, can opener, flipper
- ✓ 4 cups
- ✓ 2 medium plastic bowls
- ✓ 6-foot paper towel
- ✓ 6-foot tin foil
- ✓ sharpened filleting knife
- ✓ 2 cups cooking oil
- ✓ salt and pepper
- ✓ soft drinks or juice
- ✓ 2 eggs
- ✓ 1 cup flour
- ✓ 1 pound bacon
- ✓ 1 small tin condensed milk
- ✓ 1 tin peaches
- ✓ 1 tin luncheon meat (Oh ignominy! Oh shame!)
- ✓ 12 chocolate chip cookies
- ✓ instant coffee, tea
- ✓ sugar
- ✓ 1 beat-up old kettle
- ✓ 1 or 2 large frying pans (carried in a potato or onion sack)
- ✓ 4 large potatoes
- ✓ 1 large onion
- ✓ 1 large can baked beans
- ✓ 1 lemon (or lime)
- ✓ 8 slices bread
- ✓ ¼ pound butter
- ✓ 1 plastic garbage bag
- ✓ 3 medium-size paper bags
- ✓ leather gloves
- ✓ matches, you fool!

A green twig laid across the top of a coffee can will prevent the contents from boiling over.

The **shore lunch box** by tradition is a heavy wooden container with rope handles. Loaded with canned food, cutlery, soft drinks, and dozens of other necessities, the shore lunch box is heavy and maddeningly awkward, with sharp bottom edges that ride on the waist as it is carried on that long march down to the boat. Anglers may find that a large plastic cooler is easier to clean and lighter to haul around. Packed and organized the night before, the shore lunch box is loaded into the boat in the morning along with life preservers, fishing tackle, rain gear, and buddies.

And so the morning begins. The pursuit of gamefish is a complicated matter, and if a few words of advice could produce six or eight walleyes, you wouldn't have spent your hard-earned money on this book. Let's say that you've persuaded some rookie fishing buddies to accompany you to the same light housekeeping resort you visited last year, and after an hour or two of fishing, have discovered, to your shock and disappointment, that the walleye are no longer in any of the spots they occupied a year ago. Several hours of cruising and jigging produce one furious little sauger the size of a cigarillo. You are the guide, so the fault is yours. Eleven o'clock comes, and still no fish. The sun beats down. Your buddies are cracking crude jokes at your expense. At the bottom of the lunch box, like a trooper's last cartridge, lurks the tin of Spam. No matter where we go, there'll always be Spam.

Ten after eleven. You check out the narrows on the windward side of the lake, where the waves are chopping into a line of weeds, and right away you start catching fish. Bang. Bang. Another pass brings two more fish. By 11:45 you have released a 5 and a 6-pounder, and there are six chunky little lunch fish on the stringer. Now your pals love you. Hey, I've got another one! What fun this is! How did you know those fish were here!

Aw, it was easy.

In selecting a spot for shore lunch, guides consider wind direction, air temperature, and fire hazard. On a hot day in early summer the best place might be on the windward side of the lake, where breezes keep the guests cool and drive off insects. In autumn, it's nice to find a south-facing site on the leeward side of the lake, where it will be warm and calm. Rookie guides learn a hard lesson the first time they hold shore lunch on a beach. Ever eaten a walleye fillet battered with sand?

Upon landing, someone should be delegated to build a fire while the maestro cleans the catch. Dry branches the thickness of a finger should be used to start the fire. After the blaze is underway, wrist-thick branches are added to give the fire body. Several dozen sticks this size should be heaped alongside the fire pit for later use. The guide meanwhile has finished cleaning the fish and is washing the fillets in the lake. From the shore lunch box, he removes the condensed milk and the eggs. Cracking the eggs into a bowl, he adds one cup of condensed milk and stirs. When the eggs are stirred, the fillets are immersed in the liquid, then dropped, one at a time, into a bag containing the flour. After the bag is shaken vigorously, the fillets are coated with flour. The bag with its fully battered fillets is now put someplace where no one will step on it.

The guide, moving smartly, lays the frying pan on the fire, which has now settled somewhat, and throws in a pound of bacon. The bacon begins sizzling. Eyeing it warily, the guide commences cutting up the potatoes. At the same time, the bacon is turned when necessary. The spuds are sliced into one-inch cubes and dumped into a paper bag. The onions are sliced up also, but kept separate from the potatoes. The bacon is now finished, and the guide rips off a section of paper towel and deposits the bacon upon it, wrapping both in a sheet of tin foil to keep the bacon hot.

Add one cup of cooking oil to the bacon fat in the frying pan, and add half a dozen sticks to the fire. While the oil is heating up, open the can of beans and nestle them in the coals. Throw a tiny piece of potato into the frying

Working around a cooking fire, many guides keep leather gloves and a pair of hook-outs handy. The gloves are handy for handling hot frying pans. Hook-outs are good for retrieving hot bean cans from the fire.

pan. If bubbles boil up, the oil has reached cooking temperature. Pour all the potatoes into the frying pan and season with salt and pepper. Turn the potatoes regularly, and don't make the mistake of letting the fire die down under your frying pan. Potatoes require a hot, ambitious fire. When the potatoes are three-fourths cooked, add the onions. Onions cook faster than potatoes and both will be ready in a few minutes.

Don't try cooking over a fire until the oil is hot enough. Some fishing guides use a wooden match as a "thermostat." They throw a match into the oil. When the match ignites, the oil is hot enough to cook potatoes.

Remove the cooked potatoes and onions and wrap them in paper towel. Enclose them in a sheet of tin foil. Now add one-quarter pound of butter to the hot oil and examine your fire. The ideal fire for cooking fish consists of a bed of coals with a few wrist-thick dry branches laid on. Fish burns easily and won't need as much firewood as the potatoes. When the butter and oil are hot, lay the fillets one at a time into the pan. Lay the fillets skin side down so that they don't curl in the heat. In hot bubbling oil, fish cook quickly. After several minutes, turn the fillets once and they are done.

Lay the fillets on a paper towel and shout loudly that your friends should come and eat or you'll throw it to the gulls. By now it's probably after one o'clock in the afternoon and your buddies themselves will provide the ultimate sauce – their vicious hunger. Heap up those plates. Pull a cold drink out of the cooler, and go find a mossy ledge of granite to sit on. The calm blue waters, the trees, the clear blue sky, those puffy clouds of summer – everything somehow looks perfect when you've got a hot meal of fresh-caught Canadian fish on your knees.

And they're right when they tell you this is the best meal they've ever eaten. The last thing you want to do, on a day like this, is open a restaurant in New York City.

BAKED NORTHERN PIKE

- One 3 to 5 pound northern pike (filleted)
- cutlery and plates
- 4 ft. heavy tin foil
- 1/4 pound butter
- 1 carrot
- 2 medium potatoes
- 1 large onion
- 1 small tin tomato sauce
- 1 sharp knife
- 1 fresh lemon
- salt and pepper
- matches

Burn hearty fire of wrist-thick branches down to a bed of coals while cleaning fish. Smear tin foil generously with butter. Lay fillets on foil, along with sliced potato, carrot, and onion. Garnish with tomato sauce. Close foil envelope-style, so that juices can't leak out. Lay foil package on hot coals, and cook ten minutes per side. Serves three. Equally delicious with salmon, trout, or other fish with high body fat.

RAINY DAY CHOWDER

- Three 2 pound walleye (filleted)
- 1 large stew pot
- bowls and spoons
- 3 potatoes
- 1 large onion
- 2 carrots
- 1 can kernel corn
- 1 large can condensed milk
- 4 tablespoons butter
- salt and pepper
- matches

Light hearty fire and boil water in pot. Dice potatoes and carrots and boil until soft. Drain water. Add condensed milk. Add walleye fillets, corn, onion, and one cup drinking water. Bring to simmer. Add butter. Season and serve. Serves three to four people, and warms the heart on chilly days.

Stick smoker (left) and converted refrigerator smoker.

SMOKE *on the Water*

Once you've eaten smoked fish, prepared in the traditional style of the northern Native peoples, you'll be spoiled for life.

One blustery day in the northern Quebec Cree village of Whapmagoostui, with a hard, rain-squalling wind blowing in off Hudson Bay, I followed Annie Petagumskum along a sand dune to a row of teepees erected alongside the beach. We lifted the entrance flap of one and went inside. Two other women were cleaning fish, preparing them for smoking. A little boy named Bobby, aged two, stared at me with big eyes.

"Hi," he announced.

"Hi," I said.

Not to be outdone, he replied in a louder voice. "Hi!"

Annie Petagumskum took a hatchet and split some kindling, making a pile in the teepee's circular stone hearth. Soon a warm blaze crackled and the smoke whirled upward, drawn cleanly out the teepee's chimney. The floor was padded with an aromatic cushion of spruce boughs. The rattle of the rain and sleet against the canvas walls made this seem a perfect shelter: dry, cozy, and warm. Annie Petagumskum fixed a lattice of willow sticks to upright stakes several feet above the fire, tying the joints with bark, and laid a trio of fish on the crosspieces. One was a northern pike that might have weighed 18 pounds, fresh out of the river, but she'd trimmed away its head, guts and gills. The other two were handsome lake trout. Smoke furled and wisped around the fish. Rain scuttled on the canvas. I passed the time conducting a one-word conversation with Bobby. Eventually, Annie lifted the smoked fish off the willow lattice, and we readied ourselves for one of the finest culinary delicacies in northern Canada.

Smoked fish is regarded as a gourmet item in modern-day homes. Unfortunately, big city fire departments tend to disapprove of people building smoky fires in their backyards, so the technique of smoking fish has become something of a lost art. But in the old days, smoking was routinely used as a method of treating fish. Hardwood smoke contains microscopic quantities of chemicals like ketone and acetic acid, and as these particles are absorbed into food they destroy yeast and other bacteria. This provides an effective way of preserving perishables if you happen to live in a teepee and have no place to plug in a refrigerator.

The Ultimate Way to Freeze Fish

For years, fishing guides carefully wrapped fish fillets in brown wrapping paper before freezing. Labelled with felt pen, these fish packages would keep for two or three months before developing freezer burn.

Some genius realized that, since exposure to air causes freezer burn, fish fillets would last longer if encased in ice. By dropping a meal's worth of fillets into an empty milk carton, then filling it with water, anglers found that frozen fish would thereby last six months or longer. But have you ever tried writing "2 walleyes" on the side of a milk carton? Have you ever tried convincing a customs officer that your odd-looking milk cartons contain frozen fish?

The best way to package fish today is to use small zip-lock plastic bags. Drop one fish (two fillets) into each bag, fill it halfway with water, and then close the zipper until only a small hole remains. Squeeze the bag from the bottom until all the air has escaped, then finish locking the bag. Lay the bags flat in the freezer. Once the bag is frozen, it will form a convenient disk that can be stacked or organized in rows in the freezer. Stored this way, fish fillets will keep all winter. The sides of the package are transparent, so inspectors can see how many fillets are in each bag, and what species they are. Fishing regulations in most provinces require that you leave a small patch of skin on fillets for identifying the species. But remember, you can't have more fillets than your legal possession limit for each species.

Although most of us no longer have any practical need to smoke fish, the technique is once again becoming popular. The reason is obvious. Smoked fish and meat are, quite simply, delicious. Back in the old days, smoked fish was a much-savoured treat in the bunkhouses and trapline cabins of the Canadian woods. The best thing about smoked fish, though, is its simplicity. With only a few materials, tools, and a couple of hours' work, the modern-day angler can put together a smokehouse that produces fish every bit as scrumptious as those prized by 18th-century explorers.

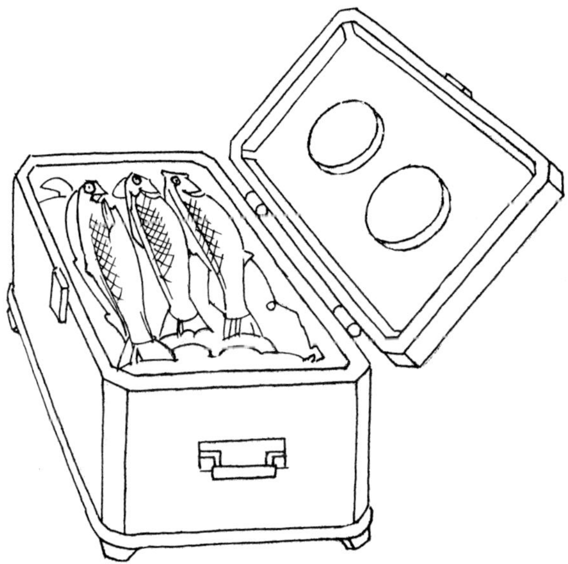

Conversations about modern-day smokehouse cuisine invariably include references to "hot smoking," "coldsmoking," "curing," and other arcane processes. Understandably, the average angler with a mess of fillets on the platter will only listen to this for a few minutes before shrugging and going back to the old frying pan. The thing to remember about smoking is that it's a simple process. Strip things down to the basics. Smokehouses fall into two main categories. Cold smokers keep the food and the fire in separate compartments. Because the fire is kept separate, the temperature in the cold smoker's food compartment generally stays below 120°F. Traditional rural smokehouses were cold smokers, and hams that hung

Curing fish or meat removes moisture and postpones deterioration. The process also adds that distinctive flavour we associate with smoked food. Meat or fish should be rolled in the curing mix and left to sit overnight in a non-metallic container. Use marinades of your own concoction as a substitute.

for days or weeks on end still required cooking afterwards. Nowadays, cold smokers have faded in popularity, and are generally used only as a means of quick-flavouring fish, like salmon, before cooking by standard methods. After all, who wants to wait for days before supper is ready?

At temperatures above 120°F, meat and fish are partially cooked as well as smoked. Treating foods by this method is called hot smoking, and it combines the flavouring of the old-fashioned method with the relatively short preparation times favoured by modern, impatient folks.

To do small fish, you don't even need a bona fide smokehouse. Let's say, for example, that you're on summer holidays with the family, and you've decided to get the kids involved in a pee-wee fishing derby. While the youngsters dig for worms, argue over fishing rods, and move from dock to dock trying to catch perch, crappies, or rock bass, you can scrounge the beach for willows and firewood. You'll need four sturdy willow stakes sharpened at one end, a dozen thin willows at least a yard long, and a bundle of dead, wrist-thick hardwood branches for the fire. Scoop out a hole in the sand and build a good, hot little campfire. Smaller pieces of wood produce coals quickly, and make a compact fire that's easier to work around. After twenty minutes you should have a thick bed of coals about the size of a stove top. Drive the stakes into the sand at the four corners of the fire to make upright posts. About knee-high above the fire, tie several willow sticks from post to post to serve as crosspieces, and build a lattice of branches upon the crosspieces. Once your lattice is finished, add a layer of green hardwood to the fire (apple, cherry, oak, willow, or other broadleaf trees). If you use birch, peel off the bark – it's very oily.

As the fish come rolling in, after you clean them, either rub the fillets in Dry Cure or merely sprinkle them with seasoning salt. Curing, remember, is just a fancy term for dipping food in salt. Soaking foods for long periods of time in brine solution, as they did in the pioneer days, is more troublesome and probably less healthy than giving them an overnight bath in marinade, or, in the case of delicate fish fillets like perch, giving them a quick roll in Dry Cure. You'll want to adjust the height of your rack so that the fish are densely surrounded by smoke but not too close to the heat of the fire. At 150°F the fish will be done in about an hour. Don't worry about checking your watch, though. When the fish begins to turn brown, press it with a fork. If it flakes cleanly, it's done. Now break out the cold drinks. Maybe the kids will even help you eat it.

There's a common misconception that fatty fishes like salmon, trout, and whitefish are the only species suitable for smoking. It's true that woodsmoke tends to desiccate. But most fish do very well with a smoke flavour, and moderately dry fish, like smallmouth and largemouth bass, or very dry fish, like walleye, can be kept moist if you baste them periodically with butter or margarine. If you're smoking bulky fish, like whole salmon, or meats in the form of a goose or venison roast, temperature control becomes more important. At this point, you may want to graduate to a home-made smokehouse or an electric smoker. These smokers do a great job on small fish too. Sometimes cutting wood, tending an open fire, and so on seems a bit too much like work.

The store-bought smokers available nowadays are simple devices, usually consisting of a metal cabinet containing a heat element in the base and a series of food racks above. You lay a pan of hardwood chips or sawdust on the heat coil, spread your bass fillets or gutted trout on the rack above, and close the door. Vents at the base control the inflow of air, and allow you to lower the temperature inside the compartment. Vents at the top allow stale smoke to exit and make a handy aperture for mounting an oven thermometer.

Home-made smokers operate on the same

Dry Cure Mix

- 2 pounds salt
- 1½ cups sugar
- 1 tablespoon black pepper
- 1 tablespoon oregano
- 1½ teaspoons onion powder

Marinade

- ½ cup pineapple juice
- 4 tablespoons lemon juice
- 2 teaspoons soy sauce
- ¼ teaspoon pepper
- 1 clove garlic

Equipment Check List:

- ✓ oven thermometer (for interior of smoker)
- ✓ meat thermometer with probe
- ✓ non-metallic bowls and containers (metal reacts with salt and imparts a bitter taste)
- ✓ basting brush
- ✓ wooden spoons and forks
- ✓ hooks and cord for hanging food in smoker

principle, but the actual appearance is limited only by the builder's imagination and skill. Architect Louis Sullivan said "every building is an act," and some anglers demonstrate that by lavishing weeks of painstaking design and labour on their smokehouse. Built of local log or stone, recessed into a glade behind the cottage or deer camp, these smokehouses speak quietly of their designer's taste. Other anglers prefer the Jed Clampett approach. They whack together smokehouses out of plywood, old steamer trunks, galvanized steel trash cans, or discarded refrigerators, arguing that such crude structures make a rustic statement of their own.

Portable store-bought smokers are widely available nowadays and, being simple and inexpensive, have become a popular item with apprentice smokehouse chefs. In any smoking system, a heat source is required, and manufactured smokers generally produce heat with a propane burner, a charcoal pan, or an electric element. For sites without electric service, a propane smoker or charcoal smoker is the obvious choice, and some excellent models are available that perform both functions. For places with electric power, an electric smoker is probably the best choice. Electric smokers are quicker than propane units. And they're safer and more user-friendly than propane units. Electric smokers have the added advantage of never running out of fuel, unless you happen to prepare dinner in the middle of a storm and the power goes off.

Electric smokers have thin metal walls and temperatures within the compartment vary considerably, depending on the season. (Never operate a smoker indoors.) At a smoking temperature of around 225°F, a decent-sized salmon, for example, is ready to eat after three hours. Instead of worrying about the length of time for each fish, though, drive a meat thermometer into the fish. When the internal temperature reaches 160°F, you've reached the point at which most meats, poultry, and stuffed fish are cooked.

It's a good idea to keep a log book for the

first few months, recording statistics on marinade, type of wood fuel, cooking times, temperature, and comments. The flavour imparted by different species of wood is a much-debated subject among chefs, and while some argue that cherry or apple woods give the best all-around performance, others prefer hickory. The average person would be hard-pressed, however, to distinguish the flavours of any of a dozen varieties of hardwood. In selecting your materials, keep an open mind and a sense of adventure. There are few rules when it comes to smoked foods. And if you run into a few snags developing your technique, be patient – it's not easy reviving a lost art.

COMPLAINT DEPARTMENT

Fish dry and leathery?
Too long in curing.

Metallic taste?
Contact with metal implements.

Bitter taste?
Smoke is too dense. Open a vent.

Mushy fish?
Fish was old or bruised.

Oily, bitter taste?
You've been using softwoods!

Sooty?
When fish clutter against each other in smoker, soot collects on surface and undersides.

DWINDLING RESOURCES

People have been quitting work early and slipping off to go fishing for four or five centuries now. But as the world's population mushrooms past the five billion mark, and natural places become fewer and more precious, conservationists are beginning to ask a legitimate question: Should we still be pestering and killing the earth's wild creatures for our own amusement?

Such a question, of course, is far too troublesome and complex to be answered with a snort of dismissal or a grumbling remark about commies and bunny-huggers. The fact is, *homo sapiens* is turning out to be the most wildly successful mammalian predator to ever come off nature's assembly line. Countless other species have met us in nose-to-nose competition and lost Big Time. Fish are included in that long roster of losers. Almost without exception, fish populations everywhere, even in Canada, are in a condition of slow and sorrowful decline.

The happy news is that anglers needn't feel necessarily apologetic, or guilty, or like they are part of the problem. In most cases, habitat destruction and commercial over-harvest are responsible for the destruction of wild fish. By joining and supporting fish-conservation groups like Trout Unlimited and Fish Futures, anglers can ensure that their hobby continues to be a positive and respectful way to use the earth's resources. Through fees devoted to conservation, licences, habitat protection,

Why do People Go Fishing?

When catch-and-release fishing first became a conservation issue, many Canadian outfitters expressed concerns that such policies would discourage tourism.

No one thought to ask tourists themselves. Recent polls of American anglers show that they fish in Canada for a variety of subjective, personal reasons. Killing fish is not a primary goal.

Question: What are the most important factors affection your enjoyment of a Canadian fishing trip? Based on a Province of Manitoba survey of 39,560 anglers the most important factors are:

1) Purity and quality of the water
2) Ability to enjoy nature's beauty
3) Escaping the daily routine
4) Being outside in nice weather
5) Gaining access to wilderness
6) Privacy
7) Catching the species we're after
8) Number of fish caught
9) Size of fish caught

anglers can actually contribute more fish to the system than they subtract.

Biologists use the term "sustainable yield" to refer to nature's habitual strategy of over-producing individuals of a species each breeding season. Whether ducks, deer, or smallmouth bass, nature hedges its bet by creating a surplus of animals on an ongoing basis. These are the ones that can be harvested by humans and other predators without dampening the core population. If the sustainable yield of 6% or 11% or 75%, depending on the species, is exceeded, then that species begins to decline.

The problem is larger than angling on the individual level: by doing our fishing at the supermarket, by buying fish that is often harvested without much consideration for annoying principles like sustainable yield, we support the continuing degradation of lakes, rivers, oceans, and the fish species they support. By allocating money to factory fish boats that strip-mine cheap food, we only hasten the day when all the world's wild species are in collapse, and humanity is face-to-face with the Final Crisis.

After four million years of heredity we are, as human beings, consumers of other life. Most of us like an occasional meal of delicious fish. And that will never change. But anglers and non-anglers are becoming more concerned about the world's dwindling resources. Instead of feeling guilty, anglers should celebrate their age-old rite of gathering life. We should teach beginners and youngsters the notions of sustainable use. Respect for living things. The interconnected web that joins all of us. We should remember to keep a few pretty ones for dinner, and let the rest go free.

How To Release Fish

In recent years, fishing has become more sport than food-gathering exercise, and with that evolution has come a strengthening of angling ethics.

Nowadays, a stringer of big fish doesn't garner compliments back at the landing. From the fly-in fishing lodges on the Arctic Circle, where anglers are no longer allowed to kill a single big fish, to the big-money fishing derbies down south, where all contenders are weighed like prize fighters, then put back in the water, catch-and-release fishing has become the leading principle of modern angling.

Ethics aside, the popularity of catch-and-release fishing also owes something to simple supply and demand. Every year, more fishing magazines, books, and TV shows hit the market. And every summer, more anglers in bigger, faster, better-equipped boats hit the water. All this angling activity has exerted pressure on fish populations, and water pollution, shoreline construction, and soil run-off have damaged fish habitat. As a result, some lakes are approaching the point of being fished out. Bruce Ranta is a biologist with the Ontario Ministry of Natural Resources, and he says that resource technicians have determined "allowable yields" for different species. "The allowable yield determines how many fish can be killed year after year without depleting stocks. In many of our largest and most important lakes, the level of harvest has been running as high as 50% above allowable yields. This will lead to the collapse of fish stocks, unless we educate people to kill fewer fish."

Occasionally anglers may debate the

merits of catch-and-release fishing, on the grounds that "they're going to die anyway." If fish are caught in deep water, or if they are bleeding, that may be true. But healthy adult fish are tough, and many biological studies have shown that survival rates for released fish are high. In some cases, large fish may be caught and released repeatedly. I know of a large female muskie that has been caught five or six times by different anglers, and one farmer from Illinois told me of a largemouth bass named Big Ralph which lives in his stock pond and, to date, has been caught and released over 30 times.

"The allowable yield determines how many fish can be killed year after year without depleting stocks. In many of our largest and most important lakes, the level of harvest has been running as high as 50% above allowable yields. This will lead to the collapse of fish stocks, unless we educate people to kill fewer fish."

To ensure that released fish survive, anglers should review their equipment and methods. Use barbless **artificial baits** if possible. Fish tend to swallow worms, minnows, and other live baits. And a fish that swallows a barbed hook is a difficult patient. If you catch a fish that's deeply hooked, cut the line instead of trying to remove the hook. The fish's digestive juices will dissolve the hook eventually, and it will stand a better chance of surviving than if you attempt surgery. You can avoid the whole issue of messy hook removals by crimping down the barbs on existing hooks. With pliers, flatten the barb until it is flush with the stem of the hook.

Fishing line should be of adequate strength (6 to 10 pound test for walleye, bass, and trout; 15 to 25 pound test for northern and muskellunge). Ultra-light line, while sporting, obliges the angler to play the fish for a long period of time, and an exhausted fish is less likely to perk up afterwards. Lake trout can be brought up from deep water without ill effect, but walleye and bass don't recover easily after being taken from water more than 40 feet deep. The pressure change causes physical trauma, evidenced by bulging eyes and protruding throats. If you're catching and releasing fish that show signs of the bends, move to shallower water.

Once subdued, a big fish like a pike or muskie is best kept in the water beside the boat. Netting tends to get those bristling hooks tangled, and the twine is rough on slime membranes. In any case, a thrashing 4-foot-long muskie doesn't belong in a boat. Stabilize the fish by gripping it behind the head. If you are curious about its weight, measure its length and girth with a tape measure or a length of cord or a piece of fishing line and determine the fish's size back on shore. Most lodges and provincial Ministry of Natural Resources departments have tables for each species, showing the weight of a fish according to its measurements. Remove the hook using a glove and pliers. Smallmouth bass, lake trout, and walleye can be lifted out of the water by net or by hand – dampen it first – and placed in a cooler half full of water to prevent them from thrashing around and injuring themselves.

Many catch-and-release anglers keep disposable cameras in their tackle box. They are handy and waterproof, and anyone who appreciates camera equipment will be disappointed to see what fine pictures they take. But if you want photographs, don't fuss. After all, if someone was taking your portrait 30 feet under the water, wouldn't you prefer they did it promptly? After returning the fish to the water, pump it gently back and forth, so that water will flow over its gills and revive it. When the fish struggles, give it a little send-off, and watch its broad tail disappear down into the depths below.

When you get back, you'll be wearing a smile, hoping someone looks at your photograph and says, "Beautiful fish. Did you let it go?"

BRITISH COLUMBIA

A feast for anglers, the province of British Columbia offers an incredible mix of opportunities, from fast-flowing mountain rivers through placid lakes and immense tidal estuaries with giant sturgeon and steelhead to the misty islands off the Pacific coast.

The province divides into a number of general regions. Vancouver Island and the Gulf Islands have good smallmouth bass and trout fishing in a number of inland lakes. Great lodges like Painters's (see "Chinook Salmon" chapter) and countless other top-notch lodges and bed-and-breakfast resorts play host to salmon anglers. The B.C. interior is a land of dry grassy plateau and boisterous, chalkboard-green rivers. Many outfitters provide float-trip services along these rivers. Up along the north coast, the rich and adventurous can take once-in-a-lifetime fishing trips by helicopter, dropping into narrow, spectacular coastal gorges where steelhead and salmon have never encountered an angler.

The province markets freshwater lodges separately from saltwater, so interested anglers should request both booklets. **Tourism British Columbia** is located at Parliament Buildings, Victoria, British Columbia, V8V 1X4. Phone: 1-800-663-6000.

Top Saltwater Lodges in British Columbia *(for Salmon and Halibut)*

April Point Lodge
PO Box 1
Campbell River, BC
V9W 4Z9
Ph: 604-285-2222

Big Spring Sport Fishing Resorts
101-4680 Cowley Cres.
Richmond, BC
V7B 1C1
Ph: 1-800-663-4400

Campbell River Lodge
1760 Island Hwy.
Campbell River, BC
V9W 2E7
Ph: 1-800-663-7212

Eagle Edge Charters
Dave Wahl
45 Braun St.
Kitimat, BC
V8C 2J1
Ph: 604-632-6530

God's Pocket Resort
PO Box 130
Port Hardy, BC
V0N 2P0
Ph: 604-949-9221

Haa-Nee-Naa Lodge
229 Pandosy St.
Kelowna, BC
V1Y 1T1
Ph: 604-763-TYEE

Hakai Beach Resort
Ste. 440
580 Hornby St.
Vancouver, BC
V6C 3B6
Ph: 604-689-9313

Hanson's Fishing Outfitters
102-580 Hornby St.
Vancouver, BC
V6C 3B6
Ph: 604-684-8988

Langara Fishing Lodge
436 W. Second Ave.
Vancouver, BC
V5Y 1E2
Ph: 604-873-4228

Pacific Rim Drift Charters
5425 Argyle St.
Port Alberni, BC
V9Y 1T6
Ph: 604-723-7438

Painter's Lodge
Oak Bay Marine Group
1327 Beach Drive
Victoria, BC
V8S 2N4
Ph: 1-800-663-7090

Rivers Lodge
George Ardley
Rivers Inlet, BC
V0C 1M0
Ph: 604-685-2127

Samson Fishing Lodge
264-810 W. Broadway
Vancouver, BC
V5Z 4C9
Ph: 604-737-2944

St. John's Fishing Lodge
Ste. 120
4977 Trennant St.
Delta, BC
V4K 2K5
Ph: 1-800-665-6020

Victory Cove Fishing Resort
Don Gillanders
PO Box 1015
Prince Rupert, BC
V8J 4H6
Ph: 1-800-665-2230

Westwind Tugboat Adventures
Capt. Bob Jordan
1160 Holdom Ave.
Burnaby, BC
V5B 3V6
Ph: 604-270-3269

Whitecap Charters
PO Box 195
Queen Charlotte, BC
V0T 1S0
Ph: 604-637-2409

Excellent Lodges on Freshwater Lakes *(for Rainbow Trout and Steelhead)*

Akehurst Lake Camp
Michael Bray
PO Box 15472
Sacramento, CA
U.S.A. 95851
Ph: 916-484-3005

Blackwater River Outfitters
Roger & Francie Lee
Box 1608
Vanderhoof, BC
V0J 3A0
Ph: 604-685-2232

Caverhill Lodge
Box 190
Barriere, BC
V0E 1EC
Ph: 604-372-6193

Chilcotin Fishing Adventures
Box 152
Whistler, BC
V0N 1B0
Ph: 604-238-2274

High Country Tourist Lodge Assoc.
2-1490 Pearson Place
Kamloops, BC
V1S 1J9
Ph: 604-372-7770

Kermode Lodge
Box 340
Smithers, BC
V0J 2N0
Ph: 604-847-4638

Moose Lake Lodge
Anahim Lake, BC
V0L 1C0
Ph: Ootsa Lake Channel H48-7487

Nimmo Bay Resort Heli-Fishing
Box 696
Port McNeil, BC
V0N 2R0
Ph: 604-956-4000

Northland Steelhead Lodge
Box 2666
Smithers, BC
V0J 2N0
Ph: 604-847-9234

Osprey Guide Services
Terry & Donna Carlyle
C-18 Sheridan Shore Site, RR #1
Lone Butte, BC
V0K 1X0
Ph: 604-593-4949

Roche Lake Lodge
Box 669
Kamloops, BC
V1S 1J9
Ph: 604-372-7770

Roche Lake Resort
Box 669
Kamloops, BC
V2C 5L7
Ph: 604-828-2007

Stewart's Lodge
Nimpo Lake, BC
V0L 1R0
Ph: 604-932-0288

Tunkwa Lake Resort
Box 196
Logan Lake, BC
V0K 1W0
Ph: 604-523-9697

Tweedsmuir Lodge
Bella Coola, BC
V0T 1C0
Ph: 604-982-2402

Tyax Mountain Lake Resort
Gold Bridge, BC
V0K 1P0
Ph: 604-238-2221

Water Ouzel Guide Service
Bob Clay
M-35, Hazelton, BC
V0J 1Y0
Ph: 604-842-6447

ALBERTA

The lakes and forest of the Canadian Shield are located in a broad belt that stretches across the entire country. Alberta is a truly western province, with cowboys and wide-open plains. Two excellent northern areas for anglers are the Peace River District and what the Alberta government calls "the Lakeland" district. The province offers brochures and information on lodges and outfitters in these regions.

Only a relatively small section of the province has an abundance of gamefish habitat. Anglers visiting Alberta therefore don't have as many opportunities as in other western provinces. But there are some important exceptions. A number of world-class trout streams run off the Rocky Mountains and drain east, across the short-grass prairie of southern Alberta. The Bow River is perhaps the most famous, with very high populations of rainbow and brown trout (see "Rainbow Trout" chapter). The Crowsnest and the Red Deer are likewise excellent streams. Many anglers believe that Alberta offers the best dry fly fishing in North America.

Alberta Tourism is located at P.O. Box 2500, Edmonton, Alberta, T5J 2Z4. Phone: 1-800-661-8888.

Lodges and Outfitters

Bar SN
Dale Hall
403 Pineridge Village
Hinton, AB
T7V 1S9
Ph: 403-865-4702

Christina Lake Lodge
Fred, Marge & Mike Thom
c/o General Delivery
Conklin, AB
T0A 0W0
Ph: 403-559-2224

Eagle River Outfitting
Reg Williams
Box 1245
Whitecourt, AB
T0E 2L0
Ph: 403-778-3251

Fawcett Lake Resort
Box 99
Smith, AB
T0G 2B0
Ph: 403-829-2301

Fort Chipewyan Adventures
Toby Taylor
Box 347
Fort Chipewyan, AB
T0B 1P0
Ph: 403-697-3679

Grist Haven Lodge
Tony Kossey
Box 1350
Grand Centre, AB
T0A 1T0
Ph: 403-594-1254

Gypsy Lake Lodge
Jeff Dodds
Box 5508
Fort McMurray, BC
T9H 3G5
Ph: 403-743-3176

Island Lake Lodge
Jim & Jen Comeau
Box 5694
Fort McMurray, AB
T9H 3G6
Ph: 403-743-0214

Lloyd Lake Lodge
Mary Jane & Richard Pliska
PO Box 6129
Fort McMurray, AB
T9H 3C6
Ph: 403-791-4042

Majic Country Wilderness
Chuck Graves
PO Box 5242
Fort McMurray, AB
T9H 3G3
Ph: 403-743-0766

Margaret Lake Lodge
Ron Laframboise
PO Box 1165
High Level, AB
T0H 1Z0
Ph: 403-659-3677

Namur Lake Lodge
Bev, Cornell & Bob Pasichnuk
PO Box 5941
Fort McMurray, AB
T9H 4V9
Ph: 403-791-9299

Northern Sport Fishing
Rod Hansen
Box 5921
Fort McMurray, AB
T9H 4V9
Ph: 403-791-3412

Sundance Lodges
Sheryl & Brian Green
Box 190
Kananaskis Village, AB
T0L 2H0
Ph: 403-591-7122

Winefred Lake Lodge
George & Ricki Maunder
c/o General Delivery
Conklin, AB
T0P 1H0
Ph: 403-551-1913

SASKATCHEWAN

The province is divided into three zones: southern, central and northern. The southern zone is mostly farmland and prairie, with numerous roads, campgrounds, and resorts, but few good fishing areas.

In Saskatchewan, the further north you go, the better the fishing. The jumping-off spot for most of the northern fly-in lodges is the town of La Ronge. Anglers often travel via scheduled airlines to Regina or Saskatoon and then connect with their outfitter upon arrival. The best way to deal with travel planning is simply to ask your outfitter to make all airline bookings and inform you of the schedule.

La Ronge is also accessible by paved highway, but beyond there roads are gravel-surfaced and services are infrequent. There are so many lakes and thick forests in northern Saskatchewan that most travel is accomplished by aircraft. The Saskatchewan Outfitters Association (Ph: 306-763-5434) provides a meet-and-greet service for visiting anglers at the Saskatoon Airport. Helpers from the association provide anglers with car rental connections, travel instructions, hotels, liaison with fishing lodges, and assorted other services.

Anglers flying in by private aircraft should contact Canada Customs (Ph: 306-780-6223) for instructions on entering Canada. Maps and aerial photos are available from Central Survey and Mapping (Ph: 306-787-2799).

The province offers many brochures, videos and travel guides from **Tourism Saskatchewan** at 1919 Saskatchewan Drive, Regina, Saskatchewan, S4P 3V7. Ph: 1-800-667-7191.

Saskatchewan's Top Lodges

(continued next page)

A & C Lodge
Jack Klassen
PO Box 8602
Saskatoon, SK
S7K 6K7
Ph: 306-253-4677

Beaver Lodge
Wallace & Elaine Johnson
Box 75
Spalding, SK
S0K 4C0
Ph: 306-872-4916

Besnard Lake Lodge
Warren Talbourdet
Box 502
Watrous, SK
S0K 4T0
Ph: 306-946-2258

Beyond LaRonge Lodge
Ron Cocojar
270 E. Adams
Saskatoon, SK
S7K 5M9
Ph: 306-242-3294

Black Bear Island Lake Lodge
Earl Mockellky
107 Wells St.
Regina, SK
S4R 6J2
Ph: 306-543-2187

Boreal Camp and Outfitting
Martin Harbicht
Box 318
La Ronge, SK
S0J 1L0
Ph: 306-425-2437

Camp Grayling
Margy Michel & Ed White
General Delivery
Stony Rapids, SK
S0J 2R0
Ph: 306-439-2188

Camp Kinisoo
Chris & Sheila Brown
Box 120
La Ronge, SK
S0J 1L0
Ph: 306-425-2024

Can-Am Outfitters
Chris & Cindy Shea
Box 1260
Brabant Lake, SK
S0J 1L0
Ph: 306-758-4898

Cree River Lodge
Bruce Anderson
Box 503
Naicam, SK
S0K 2Z0
Ph: 306-874-2355

Dore Lake Lodge
Alex & Vicky Shukin
Box 267
Big River, SK
S0J 0E0
Ph: 306-832-4511

Foster Lake Lodge
Trent Brunanski
Box 820
Wakaw, SK
S0K 4P0
Ph: 306-233-5489

Granger's Cheemo Lodge
Ed Granger
Box 248
Hardisty, AB
T0B 1V0
Ph: 403-888-2309

Hatchet Lake Lodge
George Fleming
Box 611
Postal Station G
Calgary, AB
T3A 2G5
Ph: 403-286-2717, 306-633-2132, 1-800-661-9183

Hilliard's Pine Island Camp
Butch & Neva Hilliard
Box 827
La Ronge, SK
S0J 1L0
Ph: 306-245-5173

Jim's Camp
James McKenzie
General Delivery
Mission, SK
S0J 2P0
Ph: 306-635-2052

Lawrence Bay Lodge
Randy Engen
Box 243
Tolna, ND
U.S.A. 58380
Ph: 701-262-4560

Ena Lake Lodge
Shane MacKinnon
Box 1568
Prince Albert, SK
S6V 5T2
Ph: 306-763-5558

Minor Bay Camp
Gerald Howard
Box 211
Minton, SK
S0C 1T0
Ph: 306-969-4711

Minowukow Lodge
Lu Crawford
Candle, SK
S0J 3E0
Ph: 306-929-4619

Newmart Resort
R. & M. Humen
1 Red River Road
Saskatoon, SK
S7K 1G2
Ph: 306-224-4345

Nordic Lodge
L. & D. Carlson
Box 2082
Saskatoon, SK
S7K 3S7
Ph: 306-382-0850

Northern Reflection Lodge
Eddy Jones
Box 281
Dinsmore, SK
S0L 0T0
Ph: 306-846-4509

Oliver Lake Lodge
Leonard Romaniuk
Box 99
Candle Lake, SK
S0J 3E0
Ph: 306-929-2190

Paull River Wilderness Camp
Wayne Galloway
Holbein, SK
S0J 1G0
Ph: 306-747-2862

Reindeer Lake Trout Camp
Ron Holmes
General Delivery
Southend, SK
S0L 2L0

Sportsman's Lodge
Gordon & Shirley Simpson
Box 47
Spruce Home, SK
S0J 2N0
Ph: 306-764-7471

Tazin Lake Outfitters
Harry Van der Voort
Box 238
Glendon, AB
T0A 1P0
Ph: 403-635-2596

Thunder Hills Outfitters
George Henderson
353 Kellins Crescent
Saskatoon, SK
S7N 2Y8
Ph: 306-249-2144

Trail North Fishing Camp
R. Peterson
Box 1718
Tisdale, SK
S0E 1T0
Ph: 306-873-4531

Twin Bay Resort
Greg & Debbie Seib
General Delivery
Deschambeault Lake, SK
S0P 0C0
Ph: 306-632-4767

Wollaston Lake Lodge
Brian & Sharon Elder
6000 North Douglas
Minneapolis, MN
U.S.A. 55429-9915
Ph: 1-800-328-0628

MANITOBA

At the very centre of the North American continent, Manitoba is large and relatively uninhabited, and has more lakes than any western Canadian province. While often considered a prairie province, Manitoba is heavily wooded for the most part, with a small band of agricultural prairie on the southern fringe, and several major river systems draining north towards the Arctic.

Just as Manitoba has most of western Canada's best walleye and northern pike habitat, so does it have more than its share of top-notch fishing resorts. In the south, Lake Winnipeg, the Red River, the Whiteshell, and Lake of the Prairies are popular road-accessible spots. In the north, roads are few and far between and most lodges are fly-in only. In recent years, airstrips have been installed in many of the best lodges, and anglers can connect with their flight into the lodge at Winnipeg International Airport.

For information you can write to **Travel Manitoba**, 7th floor, 155 Carleton Street, Winnipeg, Manitoba R3C 3H8. Ph: 1-800-665-0040.

Fly-In Lodges

Aikens Lake
Wilderness Lodge
G. & L. Tureene,
P. & J. Lavack
Box 98
St. Boniface PO
Winnipeg, MB
R2H 3H1
Ph: 204-237-LAKE

Amphibian Lodge
Tom Johnston
Box 975
Lac du Bonnet, MB
R0E 1A0
Ph: 204-345-8339 or
204-345-2553

Bain Lake Lodge
Jerome Fordon
Rte. 2
Sheridon, IL
U.S.A. 60551
Ph: 815-792-8594

Big Sand Lake Lodge
Don & Lynn McCrea
Room 1,
1808 Wellington Ave.
Winnipeg, MB
R3H 0G3
Ph: 204-774-6666 or
204-786-4801 ext. 7942

Bolton Lake Lodge
Brian Dick
615B Ferry Road
Winnipeg, MB
R3H 0T5
Ph: 204-772-0703 or
204-783-3000

Budd's Gunisao Lake Lodge
Jim & Brendon Budd
Box 347
596 N. Hagadorn
Mason, MI
U.S. 48854
Ph: 517-676-FISH

Burntwood Lake Lodge
Larry Gogal
Box 599
Snow Lake, MB
R0B 1M0
Ph: 204-358-2259

Cobham River Lodge
Richard Hebel
Summer: Box 143,
Stn L, Winnipeg, MB
R3H 0Z4
Winter: Box 1334,
Mason City, IA
U.S.A. 50401
Ph: 204-475-1982 or
515-423-3761

Dogskin Lake Lodge
George & Ann Maryk
Box 157
Lac du Bonnet, MB
R0E 1A0
Ph: 204-345-2972

Edmund Lake Lodge
Herb & Anna Dyke
Box 151A, RR #2
Dugald, MB
R0E 0K0
Ph: 204-444-3266 or
204-444-3426

Elbow Lake Lodge
Jack Smith
General Delivery
Wanless, MB
R0B 1T0
Ph: 204-682-7441

Fishing Lake Lodge
Byron Grapentine
Lot 46,
Antonio Road
Bissett, MB
R0E 0J0
Ph: 204-277-5262 or
204-397-9999

Gods Country Lodge
Thomas McKay
Gods River, MB
R0B 0N0
Ph: 204-366-2244

Gods River Lodge
Paul Zanowich
Box 714
Winnipeg, MB
R3C 2K3
Ph: 204-582-4937 or
204-366-2333

Harrop Lake Camp and Outpost
Scott & Gwen Compton
192 Taché Ave.
Winnipeg, MB
R2H 1Z6
Ph: 204-237-1211 or
1-800-463-4744

Fly-in Lodges

Healey's Gods Lake Narrows Lodge
John Jr., Sam & Marigold Healey
Gods Lake Narrows, MB
R0B 0M0
Ph: 204-335-2405

Island Lake Lodge
Tom Brotherston
Island Lake, MB
R0B 0T0
Ph: 204-456-2043 or
414-679-9503

Kississing Lake Lodge
Ike & Liz Enns
Summer: Box 1680,
The Pas, MB
R9A 1L5
Winter: 12000 S. 195th E. Ave.,
Broken Arrow, OK
U.S.A. 74014
Ph: 204-468-2141 or
918-455-2324 or
1-800-421-2113

Knee Lake Resort
Al Reid
Ste. 3,
1791 Dublin Ave.
Winnipeg, MB
R3H 1A9
Ph: 204-632-6098 or
U.S.A. 1-800-563-7151

Little Grand Rapids Lodge
Ernie Janzen
205-5 Donald St.
Winnipeg, MB
R3L 2T4
Ph: 204-475-9542 or
204-397-2333

Misty Lake Lodge
Peter Antsanen
Lac Brochet, MB
R0B 2E0
Phone: 204-337-2250

Molson Lake Lodge
Dianne & Lyle Fett
Norway House, MB
R0B 1B0
Ph: 701-282-7154

Munroe Lake Lodge
Lorne & Marjorie Yusishen
Box 11, Grp. 110,
RR #1C
Winnipeg, MB
R3C 2E4
Ph: 204-338-0153

Muskwa Outfitters
Ralph Merasty & Don Inglis
General Delivery
Brochet, MB
R0B 0B0
Ph: 204-323-2057 or
204-778-6182

Nejalini Lodge
Marvin H. Benson
Box 38, Grp. 347,
RR #3
Selkirk, MB
R1A 2A8
Ph: 204-284-6947 or
204-482-6884

Norse Lodge
Bob & Ruth Compton
215 E. Broadway St.
Isanti, MN
U.S.A. 55040
Ph: 612-444-4689 or
612-462-5935

Fly-in Lodges

North Country Lodge
Jack & Georgia Clarkson
General Delivery
Berens River, MB
R0B 0A0
Ph: 204-382-2379

North Seal River Lodge
Russell Baker
319 Elmhurst Road
Winnipeg, MB
R3R 0T6
Ph: 204-889-6572

Nueltin Fly-in Lodges
Garry & Lois Gurke
Summer: Box 1229,
Thompson, MB
R8N 1P1
Winter: Box 1561,
Morden, MB
R0G 1J0
Ph: 204-284-3247 or
204-822-4143

Plummer's Lodges
The Plummers
950 Bradford St.
Winnipeg, MB
R3H 0N5
Ph: 204-774-5775 or
U.S.A. 1-800-665-0240

Sasa-Ginni-Gak Lodge
Northway Aviation
Box 70
Arnes, MB
R0C 0C0
Ph: 204-642-8652

Schmerler's Gods Lake Lodge
Nelson Tomalty
Box 1708
Gimli, MB
R0C 1B0
Ph: 204-642-5216

Shining Falls Lodge
Ralph Rutledge
Box 213
Selkirk, MB
R1A 2B2
Ph: 204-785-2332 or
204-482-3270

Silsby Lake Lodge
Kip & Mickey Thompson
c/o Gold Trail Lodge
General Delivery
Ilford, MB
R0B 0S0
Ph: 204-288-4380

South Knife Lake Lodge
Gary & Sylvia Peltier
Summer: Box 310,
Thompson, MB
R8N 1M9
Winter: RR #1,
Woodlands, MB
R0C 3H0
Ph: 204-383-5230

Thunderbird Lodge
Scott & Gwen Compton
192 Taché Ave.
Winnipeg, MB
R2H 1Z6
Ph: 204-237-1211 or
U.S. 1-800-463-4744

Utik Lake Lodge & Outfitting Service
Roger Whittington & George Dram
95 Elder Bay
Thompson, MB
R8N 0Z8
or Box 100,
Wabowden, MB
R0B 1S0
Ph: 204-778-8800 or
204-689-2166

Drive-in Lodges

Webber's Lodges (Dymond Lake Lodge & North Knife Lake Lodge)
Doug & Helen Webber
Box 304
Churchill, MB
R0B 0E0
Ph: 204-675-8875 or 1-800-665-0476

Aberdeen Lodge
M. Nevakshonoff
Summer: Box 633, Flin Flon, MB
R8A 1N5
Winter: Box 427, Fisher Branch, MB
R0C 0Z0
Ph: 204-372-6913

Athapap Lodge
Stan Bowles
Box 30
Cranberry Portage, MB
R0B 0H0
Phone: 204-472-3342

Big Northern Lodge and Outfitters
John Eisner & Ian McKay
Box 279
Minitonas, MB
R0L 1G0
Ph: 204-525-4468

Big Whiteshell Lodge
Art & Ken Swirski
554 Sharron Bay
Winnipeg, MB
R2G 0H7
Ph: 204-348-7623 or 204-663-6253

Buffalo Point International Resort
Thunder Family
Box 37
Middlebro, MB
R0A 1B0
Ph: 204-437-2557 or 204-437-2133

Camp Hide Away
Garry & Kathleen McNaughton
Box 640
Lac du Bonnet, MB
R0E 1A0
Ph: 204-345-2566

Caribou Lodge
Gervais & Martha Beaulleu
Box 231
Cranberry Portage, MB
R0B 0H0
Ph: 204-472-3351

Caribou Lodge on Quesnel Lake
Maurice Sala
Box 171
St. Germain, MB
R0G 2A0
Phone: 204-254-8400

Carpenter's Clearwater Lodge
D. & K. Sangster, J. & S. Lorden
Box 695
The Pas, MB
R9A 1K7
Ph: 204-624-5467

Chesley's Lodge and Resort
Bruce & Ingrid McLay
Box 2
Petersfield, MB
R0C 2L0
Ph: 204-738-2250

Cormorant Lodge
Ed Buchik
Summer: General Delivery, Cormorant, MB
R0B 0G0
Winter: 1308 Portage Avenue, Winnipeg, MB
R3G 0V2
Ph: 204-357-2171 or 204-889-2171

Crowduck Lake Camp
Nick & Bill Kolansky
Box 502
Portage la Prairie, MB
R1N 3B9
Ph: 204-239-6976

Drive-in Lodges

Eagle Nest Lodge
Fred & Jo-Anne Pedruchny
Box 25
Pointe du Bois, MB
R0E 1N0
Ph: 204-884-2301 or
U.S.A. 1-800-665-0232

Grass River Lodge
Ike & Liz Enns
Summer: Box 1680,
The Pas, MB
R9A 1L5
Winter: 12000 S. 195th E. Avenue,
Broken Arrow, OK
U.S.A. 74014
Ph: 204-358-7171 or
U.S.A. 1-800-421-2113
or 918-455-2324

Inverness Falls Resort
Stuart & Judy Cornell
Rennie P.O.
Rennie, MB
R0E 1R0
Ph: 204-369-5336

Jessica Lake Lodge
Bill & Laurie Scarfe
Rennie, MB
R0E 1R0
Ph: 204-348-7544

Kendall Point Lodge
Garth & Darren Deason
Summer: Box 71,
Pointe du Bois, MB
R0E 1N0
Winter: 53 Berrydale Avenue
Winnipeg, MB
R2M 1M1
Ph: 204-884-2327 or
204-255-1548

Lake Manitoba Narrows Lodge
Stasiuk family
Oakview P.O.
Lake Manitoba Narrows, MB
R0C 2K0
Ph: 204-768-2749

New Vickery Lodge
Rick & Fran Hubbs
Box 2670
The Pas, MB
R9A 1M5
Ph: 204-624-5429

Nopiming Lodge
Marge & Blaine Guenther
Box 723
Lac du Bonnet, MB
R0E 1A0
Ph: 204-884-2281

North Star Tourist Camp
Waterhen Band Development Corp.
Waterhen, MB
R0L 2C0
Ph: 204-628-3462

Nutimik Lodge
Edna Kuhn & Janet Wilson
Box 40
Seven Sisters Falls, MB
R0E 1Y0
Ph: 204-348-7652 or
204-348-2669

Peterson's Reed Lake Lodge
Kathy & Corky Petersen
Summer: Box 1648,
The Pas, MB
R9A 1L4
Winter: 214-956 Chancellor Drive,
Winnipeg, MB
R3T 2K1
Ph: 204-261-8176

Drive-in Lodges

Pine Grove Cabins
Gib & Audrey Hobbs
Box 2
Grand Rapids, MB
R0C 1E0
Ph: 204-639-2266

Pine Island Lodge
Brian Burgess
Box 3, Station L
Winnipeg, MB
R3H 0Z4

Ptarmigan Motor Lodge
Bill & Anne Berg
Box 29
Cranberry Portage, MB
R0B 0H0
Ph: 204-472-3285

Redwood Inn
Cyril Perry
Sherridon, MB
R0B 1L0
Ph: 204-468-2007 or 204-468-2017

Tall Timber Lodge
George Maryk
Box 157
Lac du Bonnet, MB
R0E 1A0
Ph: 204-345-2972 or 204-345-9375

Trailhead Cabin
Anne Schuster
Box 14
Lake Audy, MB
R0J 0Z0
Ph: 204-848-7649

Trapper Don's Lodge and Outfitting
Don & Lynn McCrea
Box 44
Cowan, MB
R0L 0L0
Ph: 204-569-4833 or 204-569-4804

Viking Lodge
Ted Smith
Box 190
Cranberry Portage, MB
R0B 0H0
Ph: 204-472-3337

Wally's Place
Gene & Karen Assailly, Wally & Shirley Nicklin
Box 56
Gerald, SK
S0A 1B0
Ph: 204-546-9936 or 306-745-2378

Wellman Lake Lodge & Outfitters
Alvin & Linda Wiebe
Box 249
Minitonas, MB
R0L 1G0
Ph: 204-525-4422

Wekusko Falls Fishing Lodge
Ted Stabback & Dwayne Brew
PO Box 705
Snow Lake, MB
R0B 1M0
Ph: 204-358-2341 or 204-358-2270 or 204-358-7144

Windsock Lodge
Tim & Donna Hastings
General Delivery
Bissett, MB
R0E 0J0
Ph: 204-257-8215

Wolverine Lodge
Renee & Fred Bettschen
Summer: Box 189,
Lynn Lake, MB
R0B 0W0
Winter: Box 2206,
Palm Springs, CA
U.S.A. 92263
Ph: 1-800-356-PIKE

NORTHWESTERN ONTARIO

This part of Canada is a geographical oddity. Technically part of Ontario, it is nevertheless 1000 miles west of the provincial capital and most residents of this part of Ontario feel closer, physically and politically, to western Canada than the east.

Northwestern Ontario is dominated by the Precambrian Shield, so it has thousands of wilderness lakes and rivers. Likewise, there are more fishing camps here than in any other province. Dominant species in Northwestern Ontario are pike, walleye, and bass. A small but dedicated angling fraternity pursue muskellunge. Most visitors to Northwestern Ontario drive in. There are good highways that deliver anglers to the heart of fishing country. Those with the financial resources can take float planes further into the back country.

For a complete list of lodges in northwestern Ontario, contact the **Northern Ontario Tourist Outfitters Association**, Box 1140, North Bay, Ontario, P1S 8K4. Phone 705-472-5552.

Some Excellent Northwestern Ontario Lodges

Amik Lodge
Barry & Brett Arnason
Box 48, Group 200, RR #2
Winnipeg, MB
R3C 2E6
Ph: 204-633-2567

Big Hook Wilderness Camp
The Hartles
Box 1342
Red Lake, ON
P0V 2M0
Ph: 414-457-3525

Bull Moose Camp
The Metzners
Box 1009
Red Lake, ON
P0V 2M0
Ph: 807-773-1080

Camp Midgard
Manfred Mueller
General Delivery
Savant Lake, ON
P0V 2S0
Ph: 807-584-2237

Camp Quetico
Marshall & Karen Manns
Box 1087
Atikokan, ON
P0T 1C0
Ph: 807-929-2266

Deer Path Lodge
Robert & Janis Young
Box 99
Sioux Lookout, ON
P0V 2T0
Ph: 807-737-1050

Flindt Landing Camp
David Gish
General Delivery
Savant Lake, ON
P0V 2S0
Ph: 807-584-2200

Gunn Lake Lodge
Sally Kendall & Kelly Gibson
General Delivery
Minaki, ON
P0X 1J0
Ph: 807-224-2321

Halley's Camp
Gene & Wanda Halley
PO Box 15
Minaki, ON
P0X 1J0
Ph: 807-224-6531 or 1-800-465-3325

Hanson's Wilderness Lodges
The Hansons
Box 96
Nestor Falls, ON
P0X 1K0
Ph: 807-484-2115

Lac Seul Lodge
Don & Rhonda McDonald
Box 517
N. Ear Falls, ON
P0V 1T0
Ph: 807-222-2107

Laughing Waters Lodge
Rob & Barb Madden
P.O. Box 7
Sioux Narrows, ON
P0X 1N0
Ph: 807-226-5212

Some Excellent Northwestern Ontario Lodges

Mead's Spruce Island Camp
Suzy Mead
Box 19
Kenora, ON
P9N 3X1
Ph: 807-543-4087

Minaki Lodge
Four Seasons
Box 26
Minaki, ON
P0X 1J0
Ph: 807-224-4000

Pickerel Arm Camp
The Edwardsons
Box 458
Sioux Lookout, ON
P0V 2T0
Ph: 807-737-2499

Red Indian Lodge
Herb & Mary Anne Hoffman
Box 270
Sioux Narrows, ON
P0X 1N0
Ph: 1-800-465-1093

Tip Top Lodge
Jack Barta
1612 No Bell
Freemont, NE
U.S.A. 68025
Ph: 402-359-2309

About the Illustrator

Luther Pokrant has lived most of his life in Manitoba and is inspired by the lake and bush areas of the province and the many moods created by water. The surface of a pond becomes a float plane made interesting by changing configurations of shadows and reflections. Floating water lilies are colours on a painter's palette.

Born in 1947 in southern Manitoba, he received a B.F.A. degree from the University of Manitoba School of Art and an M.A. degree from New Mexico State University. Specializing in drawing and art history, his work includes thematic and historical illustration of a composite nature. Portraiture, often of other artists and their work, as well as the creative process itself, are subjects that continue to interest him.

Selected collections include the Canada Council Art Bank, Manitoba Government, Parks Canada, City of Winnipeg, Canadian External Affairs Department, Winnipeg Art Gallery, Faculty of Law and St. John's College (University of Manitoba), Shell Canada, British Petroleum, Bronfman Collection, Health and Welfare Canada, Sask Tel, Sask Oil, Arctic Trading Co., Rowing Canada, Alliance for Life, Cargill Grain, Coopers & Lybrand and Canadian Imperial Bank of Commerce.

Luther Pokrant is currently represented by Loch Mayberry Gallery in Winnipeg, Assiniboia Gallery in Regina, and Canadian Art Gallery in Calgary.

About the Author

Jake MacDonald is a full-time writer who spends his summers in a floating cedar house on the Winnipeg River. Over the past 20 years, he has also worked as a fishing guide in Northwestern Ontario. His stories appear frequently in magazines such as *Outdoor Canada*, *Canadian Geographic*, *Field and Stream* and *Cottage Life*. He is the author of several works of fiction, including *The Bridge Out of Town* and *Raised by the River*. "I often focus on the lives of people who live in small wilderness communities. Many of them make their livings as lodge operators and fishing guides." *Lakes, Lures and Lodges* is his fifth book.